Windows
ON THE
Future

D1503094

We dedicate this book to our wives and children.

Ted McCain · Ian Jukes

Windows
ON THE
Future

EDUCATION in the
Age of Technology

CORWIN PRESS, INC.
A Sage Publications Company
Thousand Oaks, California

For information:

Corwin Press, Inc.
A Sage Publications Company
2455 Teller Road
Thousand Oaks, California 91320
E-mail: order@corwinpress.com

Sage Publications Ltd.
6 Bonhill Street
London EC2A 4PU
United Kingdom

Sage Publications India Pvt. Ltd.
M-32 Market
Greater Kailash I
New Delhi 110 048 India

Printed in the United States of America

Library of Congress Cataloging-in-Publication Data

McCain, Ted D. E.
  Windows on the future : Education in the age of technology / by
Ted McCain and Ian Jukes.
    p. cm.
  Includes bibliographical references and index.
  ISBN 0-7619-7711-2 (cloth: alk. paper)
  ISBN 0-7619-7712-0 (pbk.: alk. paper)
  1. Education—Data processing. 2. Educational innovations.
  I. Jukes, Ian. II. Title.
LB1028.43 .J85 2000
370'9—.285—dc21   00-008956

This book is printed on acid-free paper.

  02   03   04   05   06   07   7   6   5   4   3

Corwin Editorial Assistant: Kylee Liegl
Production Editor: Denise Santoyo
Editorial Assistant: Candice Crosetti
Typesetter/Designer: Cristina Hill
Indexer: Teri Greenberg

Contents

Foreword   vii
  David D. Thornburg, Ph.D.

Acknowledgments   x

About the Authors   xii

Introduction   1

1. Window 1: The Power of Paradigm   13

2. Window 2: Mounting Paradigm Pressure   21

3. Window 3: Assessing Your Paradigm   25

4. Window 4: The Technology of Change   33

5. Window 5: Moore's Law   45

6. Window 6: Looking at the Road Ahead   51

7. Window 7: It Is Time for Education to Catch Up   67

8. Window 8: Education in the Future   77

9. Window 9: New Skills for Students   91

10. Window 10: New Roles for Educators   113

11. Window 11: The Need for Vision   123

Recommended Readings   129

References   137

Index   139

Foreword⨼

As frequent speaker at conferences throughout the United States and Canada, I was bound to encounter Ted and Ian sooner or later. It was sooner, and it has been my pleasure to see, hear, and collaborate with these two thinkers for more than a decade. Together, we have traveled far and wide and have spoken at conferences from Alaska to Florida and most places in between. We have lost luggage together, faced the terror of equipment failure minutes before major presentations, and have gotten into the kind of trouble that makes for good stories (but not, fortunately, for this book). The authors of this book are, like many gifted speakers, larger than life. They exhort, cajole, plead, and inform audiences throughout the United States and Canada for one simple reason: They believe that schools need to meet the needs of children and that the educational systems of our respective countries are out of whack with reality.

Like all who live by the crystal ball, Ted and Ian have modified their perspectives on technology many times as reality outstripped projections that (at the time) seemed to be "far out." This is a common dilemma faced by anyone trying to make sense of the world of technology as it applies to learning. Just as you are being criticized for "pie in the sky" futuristic thinking, the headline of a morning paper announces the release of a technology that you thought would take another few years to come to market. Futurism is a dangerous craft, especially if it wanders into the domain of forecasting. This is why we look for touchstones such as Moore's Law (described in the following chapters) and other rules of thumb that use history as a basis for extrapolations that appear too fantastic for words on one hand yet are reasonable projections of where we might be in the future.

Although the technologies they have talked about over the years have changed, their underlying ideas have not: The challenge is not to think about changes in the technology itself (although you will see plenty of that in this volume), it is to think about the transformations of education that can be facilitated by the effective use of this tech- nology. The transformations of our systems of learning deserve our attention, not the technologies that can facilitate this change. I am not a believer in technological determinism (a good thing, given how slowly schools have adopted information technology into their core structures). I do believe, however, that tools known to have value for learning outside of school (namely home and work) should be used more effectively in the place where learning is the only job: school. McCain and Jukes concur.

Ted and Ian call for dramatic changes with a fervor that acknowl- edges how far we have to go just to catch up with the world outside of school. I share their concern while heeding the advice of my col- league, Paul Saffo, who reminds me never to mistake a clear view for a short distance. Can we envision a different kind of schooling? Of course, and Ted and Ian do so in this book. Can we change our insti- tutions to reflect these changes? Of course—they are human inven- tions and therefore subject to adaptation by humans. Will we have the courage to make the changes needed to bring educational prac- tice in line with the needs of 21st-century learners? It turns out, in my opinion, that this is an interesting but not essential question. I truly hope that we will have the courage to make these changes, but if we do not, our children will still be well served—just not by their old schools. Schools that fail to adapt to the needs of the society in which they exist will simply go out of existence, replaced by new educa- tional institutions funded by the public or private sector. The initial move will probably come from corporate sponsorship, either in the form of new private educational institutions (some of them Web based) created by new companies to meet the need or, in the form of schools created by corporations who are driven into the education field because their employees lack the skills they need to thrive in the world of work. (This has already happened at the college level with institutions such as Motorola University, which plans to open another campus or two in mainland China.) If this view appears far fetched, one need look only back as far as Horace Mann to see how his model of the common school dovetailed with the needs of Massachusetts employers in the 1800s.

Do I care how this all plays out? Yes, of course I do. Education is far more than training. In the United States, it is the primary means through which people learn to take part in the running of a democracy. Personally, it would be tragic if educators were to ignore some of the points made in this book—if they were to continue to "Yes, but—" themselves into the next century.

This book you hold contains some simple yet powerful ideas. As you read, you will learn how to "live life like a quarterback" and that how we use technology is (as I like to put it) more important than *if* we use technology.

Ted and Ian have provided a map—not the only map by any means but a map just the same. The challenge is up to you. How will you use their map? What will you see when you gaze through their windows on the future? Most important, what concrete actions will you take as a result of reading this book?

With these questions in mind, I send you on an adventure to get a highly personal perspective on ways that education can take advantage of technology—an adventure presented by two of the more popular presenters in this field. I hope you enjoy the trip as much as I did.

—*David D. Thornburg, Ph.D.*

⌐Acknowledgments

We would like to thank those people who gave us the benefit of their wisdom, experience, and time. In particular, we would like to thank Kate Matheson, Bruce Macdonald, and Gail McDermott, who meticulously edited the manuscript more times than we wish to admit. Special thanks to Anita Dosaj for suggesting the title of this book.

In addition, Corwin Press would like to acknowledge the contributions of the following reviewers:

Frank Buck
Graham School
Talladega, Alabama

Shirley Campbell
University of Pittsburgh
Pittsburgh, Pennsylvania

Wanda M. Haight
Alvarado Middle School
Union City, California

Paul G. Preuss
The Herkeimer BOCES
Herkeimer, New York

Karen L. Tichy
Catholic Education Office, Archdiocese of St. Louis
St. Louis, Missouri

⌐About the Authors

Ted McCain worked for several years in the computer industry as a programmer, salesperson, and consultant before entering the teaching profession. In education, he has been a teacher, administrative assistant, and technology consultant. He is currently the coordinator of instructional technology for Maple Ridge Secondary School in Vancouver, British Columbia, and also teaches computer networking, graphic design, and desktop publishing for Okanagan College. In addition, he is the author of six books on the future, educational technology, and graphic design.

Ted McCain is a recipient of the 1997 Prime Minister's Award for Teaching Excellence. In addition to his work as an educator, for the past 20 years Ted has also consulted with businesses and school districts on the purchase and implementation of computer systems. He has given many presentations and workshops on the business and educational uses of computers. His clients have included Apple Computer, Microsoft, Aldus, and Toyota, as well as many school districts and educational associations in both Canada and the United States. He has now joined the Thornburg Center for Professional Development in San Carlos, California as an associate director. In this role, he has expanded his work as a technological and educational futurist. He focuses on the impact of the astounding changes taking place in the world today as a consequence of technological development, and is passionate in his belief that schools and communities must change so that they can effectively prepare students for the rest of their lives. His presentations emphasize the need for parents, teachers, businesses, and community members to act differently to prepare students in today's schools for the technologically rich future they will undoubtedly face.

Ian Jukes has been a teacher, administrator, writer, consultant, university instructor, and keynote speaker. As the Director of the InfoSavvy Group, he works extensively with school districts, businesses, community organizations, and other institutions to help shape preferred futures. He is the creator and codeveloper of TechWorks, the internationally acclaimed K-8 technology framework. Together with Anita Dosaj, Jukes was the catalyst behind the NetSavvy and InfoSavvy information literacy series, and is a contributing editor for both *Audio Education Journal* and *Technology and Learning* magazine. He recently published *Net.Savvy, Second Edition: Building Information Literacy for the Classroom*, coauthored with Anita Dosaj and Bruce Macdonald.

Ian Jukes is an educator first and foremost. His focus has consistently been on the compelling need to restructure our institutions so that they become relevant to the current and future needs of children. His rambunctious, irreverent, and highly charged presentations emphasize many of the practical issues related to ensuring that change is meaningful. As a registered educational evangelist, his self-avowed mission in life is to ensure that children are properly prepared for their future rather than for society's past. As a result, his perspectives tend to focus on many of the pragmatic issues that provide the essential context for educational restructuring. Fasten your seat belts and strap on your cerebral flak jacket. Counseling can and will be provided.

CORWIN
PRESS

The Corwin Press logo—a raven striding across an open book— represents the happy union of courage and learning. We are a professional-level publisher of books and journals for K–12 educators, and we are committed to creating and providing resources that embody these qualities. Corwin's motto is "Success for All Learners."

Introduction⏋

Change is a subtle thing. Change is sneaky. Although most of us are aware that *something* has changed in our lives, it is often very difficult to put our finger on exactly *what* has happened, *how* things have changed, or *why* things are different. What puts this into perspective for us is our children. We do not *see* them grow, but they do, right before our very eyes. It is only when we are confronted by the fact that their clothes or shoes do not fit any more or when we compare them with the photos we took mere weeks or months ago that we become aware of the magnitude of the changes that are taking place right before our very eyes. It is difficult to accept that these are the same little

Change is an amazing thing. We do not notice it occurring until one day we turn around and cannot believe what has happened.

ones who used to fall asleep in our arms, and it is hard for us to see the change because they are in front of our faces all the time.

Change happens much the same way in our lives. The world we live in today is really a different place from the world we lived in even a few short years ago. Although it is sometimes difficult to see this in perspective, these are truly amazing times. We live in a world where change has become the constant. Hard as it may be to accept, 10 years from now, today's world will have re-created itself many times. Even if we are able to tune into the fact that the world is changing rapidly, it is almost impossible to quantify and qualify the scope and scale of the changes that we are experiencing.

As a result, many of the personal coping strategies we have learned over the years to deal with change have begun to unravel. In fact, they probably began to fail us several years back—we just did not see that this was happening. If the coping strategies we used a decade ago are not working well now, it is almost a certainty that they will be completely useless as we plunge into the 21st century. The only way we can hope to survive the impending tempest of change is to learn the art of the chameleon: to master change until we are able to move in concert with changes as they occur.

This book can help. It contains a number of ideas and strategies developed from hundreds of presentations that have been delivered to thousands of educators, administrators, and business and professional people throughout North America.

We believe that there is a simple formula for coping with change. At the very center of it all, the key issue is our mind-set or paradigm. *Paradigm* determines how well we handle changes. Dealing with change requires us to cultivate a unique set of attitudes and skills that are necessary if we are to successfully leverage the changes for our benefit. Our journey begins here because it is paradigm that most often prevents us from acknowledging change, as well as developing the attitudes and skills needed to deal with it. Once we begin to understand the ways in which our paradigm talks to us (and how it can even paralyze us), we will be able to interpret change from a variety of perspectives.

This book will also analyze a number of key trends that will most certainly affect every aspect of our lives in the new millennium. By assessing our paradigms and using our understanding of the ways in which the world is changing, we can begin to develop the new skills and new strategies that will be needed to thrive in the 21st century.

It is important for the reader to understand from the outset that we do not worship at the altar of technology. We do not suffer from terminal "technodrool" or "technolust" (well, maybe just a little). We are educators first and foremost and are technologists only as a distant second. As a consequence, this book is not about cards and cables, hardware and software, input and output, or even RAM and ROM. Instead, this book is about change. It must be clearly understood that technology is at the heart of most of the change we now experience. For many problems that exist in the world, there are technology-based solutions for dealing with them. However, having access to the technology and being able to cope with the changes it creates are two fundamentally different issues. We must distinguish between the available technology and the mind-set that directs its use. In a world of constant change, unprepared people often become uncomfortable and disoriented. Uncomfortable people will do almost anything to become comfortable again, including turning away from change and giving in to the lure of the familiar.

The Lure of the Familiar

We will admit right up front that we are both charter members of a group known as Overusers Anonymous. One of us has a leather jacket that was bought many years ago during the university years. That jacket is a much loved piece of clothing and is still worn today, more than 20 years later, any time the opportunity arises—despite the fact that the jacket has definitely seen better days. It has rips and stains, it is out of style, and it just doesn't seem to fit the way it used to. So what? When people comment about how shabby it is, he just tells them that it is not old, it has character! Sadly, others do not seem to share this perspective. In fact, the condition of the jacket has deteriorated to the point where his wife has warned him that if he ever leaves the property again wearing it, she will personally incinerate it, probably with him in it!

Yet despite all of these dire threats, he just cannot seem to bring himself to get rid of it or buy another one. Why? Because that old jacket is just so darn comfortable. Besides, it took so long to break it in that the thought of going through that process again with a new coat is just too unsettling. He would rather put up with incredulous looks when wearing that old jacket than go out and buy a new one.

The problem is that it took a lot of hard work to make that jacket comfortable. He knows that he can afford to buy a new one, but he does not want to. If he bought a new one, he would have to start all over again from scratch, and getting comfortable with it would take time. Consequently, he is reluctant, some might suggest resistant, to making what his wife and friends believe is an absolutely necessary change.

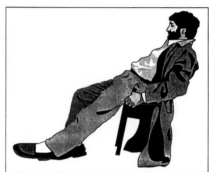

Once effort has been spent to break things in, the level of comfort we have with items such as a favorite old jacket make us resistant to change.

Why Does He Do This?

At first we thought it was just his own personal problem, but we have since discovered that most people have items somewhere in their lives that have become so comfortable they just cannot seem to part with them. For some, it is a favorite piece of furniture that has seen better times. Most of us know someone who owns a tattered old couch that has descended slowly down the feeding chain from the living room to the den to the basement and out into the garage where it sits, like an old friend, waiting to embrace us. Others cannot change the color of their house, replace the carpet, or get rid of their faithful old car. For most of us, these are special items that have significant personal meaning. It is human nature to cling to what is familiar and comfortable.

However, old coats and favorite chairs are not the only things that provide us with comfort. We also become attached to ideas, certain ways of doing things, and even views of the world. These mental patterns can become like an old coat; they make no great demands on us. Once we have invested the initial effort in making an idea our own, it is very easy to avoid dealing with changes that may force us to embrace new or different ways of thinking. Just look at the difficulty people had in accepting that the world was round or that the earth revolved around the sun. Change is consistently resisted because it represents work and is often seen as a threat to our comfort level.

Coming to Terms With Technology

Technological development often forces change, and change is uncomfortable. This is one of the main reasons why technology is often resisted and why some perceive it as a threat. It is important to understand our natural aversion to being uncomfortable when we consider the impact of technology on our lives. If truth be known, most of us prefer the path of least resistance. This tendency means that the true potential of new technologies may remain unrealized because, for many, starting something new is just too much of a struggle. Even our ideas about how new technology can enhance our lives may be shaped or limited by this natural desire for comfort. So the first lesson and the key to dealing with technology is to learn how to discriminate between the technology and the ideas that guide its use.

Technology changes the way things are done. It pushes us out of our comfort zone, so its use is naturally resisted.

Our Changing View of Computers

One way to see how a primary focus on hardware gives us an incomplete picture of the true impact of technology is to look at the way the computer industry has changed since the 1970s. If we had first become involved in computing at a university in the mid-1970s, we would have worked on a mainframe computer, likely made by IBM, Burroughs, or DEC. We would have accessed the computer remotely, using punched cards to enter our programs. Our output would have been a printout. Strangely, particularly from the perspective of today, we would never have seen the computer we were working on. In fact, we would not even have been allowed to go into the computer center where the computer was housed, mainly for reasons of security and cleanliness. In addition, the machine we used to do our computing would have then been worth many millions of dollars and would have occupied an entire floor of a building.

By the late 1970s, computers had become much less expensive and much smaller than the big mainframes. There were minicomputers that could be housed completely in a large room. The cheapest machine we could have found would have been a Wang computer with 64K of memory. This was a bargain for $151,000! The terminals, disk drives, and printers were all add-on costs, of course (so what's changed?): A terminal was $2,200, a disk drive was $38,000, and a printer was $26,000 (yes, these are actual prices!). As a result, minicomputers, although smaller and cheaper than mainframes, were still quite large and relatively expensive.

By 1979, a remarkable change was occurring. Microcomputers had finally developed into workable systems. They came complete with the necessary peripheral devices and business software to perform business tasks. The price of an entire system, including computer, screen, keyboard, disk drive, printer, and software, was only $5,000 to $6,000. As a result, sales of microcomputers absolutely skyrocketed when businesses discovered these small and relatively inexpensive devices. The sudden appearance of such powerful computer technology in business and education led many to believe that we were in the middle of a computer revolution.

Since then, the microcomputer has invaded more aspects of life than anyone could ever have anticipated in 1979. How could we ever have imagined that computers and embedded microprocessors

Consider the advances in power
and utility that have appeared
during the past 40 years in the
development of computers. In the
1950s, computers took up entire
floors of buildings. Today, we can
carry under our arm more power
than one of those behemoths.

would one day control virtually every aspect of life from laptops to
Trident missiles, VCRs, and sprinkler systems? Today, the microcomputer revolution is an accepted fact, but with the amazing
increase in the capabilities of these machines, combined with the
astounding rate at which new developments are being brought to
the market and the remarkable drop in the cost of technological
power, it is all too easy to make the technology the focus of our attention. This tendency must be resisted at all costs, however, because to
focus on hardware without fully grasping the long-term implications of the application of that technology can lead to some dangerous and crippling consequences.

Stepping Back From Technology

It is hard for us to gain a realistic perspective about technology
primarily because it is always right there in front of us. It is like putting your outspread hand in front of your eyes. You can see a few
things in the distance through the gaps between your fingers, but
your hand is mostly what you see. To get a better perspective of
things, you must move your hand back so your focus can shift to the
larger picture. To gain a realistic perspective about technology, it is
critical that we stand back from the technology sitting on our desks
and consider how that technology fits into the bigger picture of modern life. The critical issues we face do not relate specifically to the
technology but, rather, to the context in which the technology is
viewed and used. Where does technology fit? How can/should it be
appropriately and effectively used? To gain this perspective, we
must appreciate that technology is not the central issue. When used
appropriately, technology is little different from a pen. Pens are
transparent. We do not ponder the pen; we simply use it. In fact,
most of us do not even think about the pen when we use it unless it

runs out of ink or we cannot find it. It is not the pen, but what we *use* the pen for that is the critical point.

We should endeavor to think about technology in much the same way. To do this, we must conceive of new ways of thinking about technology, taking into account the human world. In taking this perspective, we can allow the technology to slip into the background and focus on what the technology does to and for people. Only when the technology becomes transparent and disappears into the background will we be able to use it without thinking. In doing so, we can move beyond the technology to new and far more important goals.

We are certainly not there yet. For example, we still marvel at powerful notebook computers with enormous storage capacity, blazing speed, and access to the worldwide information network. We still focus on the technology, not on what it can do. We often fail to grasp the significance of the interconnection. Stepping back, we must understand that carrying an expensive laptop computer is like owning just one very important book in an enormous library, and that the power of the information in this library has the potential to greatly change our lives.

Only by distancing ourselves from a primary focus on the technology can we examine the changes taking place from a much broader perspective. A revolution in the sales of computers and in the capabilities of these devices does not mean that there will be a simultaneous revolution in the way people live or think. Just because we have access to the boxes does not mean that anything of real significance is happening. To understand this, we need go no further than to look at how computers are being used today. In business, computers are used for computerized accounting, record keeping, and the production of paper-based communications. In education, many computers are still being used for simple drills and practice of skills without any context for these skills, but there is nothing revolutionary about this. For the most part, computers are still being used to reinforce old ways of doing things—we simply have powerful new devices that allow us to do this work faster and more efficiently.

Rethinking Technology

We must ask ourselves the following critical question: Is technology really changing our lives in fundamental ways, or is it merely being used to speed up old and outdated ways of doing things? (Are we doing fundamentally different things or just doing the same old things a little differently?) Although computers can now use sound, video, text, and graphics, for many users, their computers are not yet full-blown multimedia computers, primarily because the computer screen still demands the focus of our attention rather than fading into the background. The reason for this is that the use of new technology is being guided by the old mental patterns we developed before we encountered these new devices. Just like the prospect of discarding an old coat, we resist the changes that result from the introduction of new innovations. Consequently, the changes that do take place are guided by old ways of thinking because the prospect of having to change our thinking is unsettling. This is a critical point: It is not that changes are not taking place; it is that these changes are not as substantial as they could or should be simply because our human nature tries to minimize the discomfort that results from the use of new technologies.

As David Thornburg said in his speech at the Computer Using Educators of California Conference, October 1997, "when traveling at the speed of light, you don't need a rear view mirror." This may be true, but for many of us, when changes happen quickly we tend to hang on to old ideas and subconsciously look back. When we do this, we limit our ability to change. It is time to rethink this approach.

We need to rethink what is really important in the use of technology. Amazingly, it is not the technology but the people who use it and their mind-sets that are the critical determining factors.

Only recently have there been signs that the microcomputer technology developed in the late 1970s is beginning to fundamentally alter our lifestyles. Some big changes are happening, such as telecommuting and the flattening of organizational hierarchies. The fact that it took nearly 20 years for these changes to begin is a telling point. This time lag is a natural human response to new developments, even potentially life-changing technologies. It takes time for people to wrap their heads around new ideas and feel some level of comfort with the changes resulting from new technologies. So in terms of everyday life and despite all the rhetoric and hype, it is more likely that there has been a computer evolution than that there has been a computer revolution.

⌐ So What Is the Problem?

As we enter the new millennium, it appears that people are slowly beginning to understand the true potential of new technology. Although this lags significantly behind the introduction of new developments, we are beginning to see a new way of life gradually appear. More and more people are becoming comfortable with the new technologies. If this is the case, what is the problem? Why write a book about it? Actually, there are several reasons.

First, technology-driven change is growing rapidly in power and speed. As a result, increasingly there is less time to get used to bigger and bigger changes in our lives. The reality is that most of us no longer have the necessary time to get comfortable with new technology at our leisure.

Second, we cannot look at the impact of technology on our lives in isolation from the effect it has on the rest of the world. Today, no country is an island and therefore exempt from the changes brought on by new devices. Communication technology has shrunk our world to the point where we truly live in a global village where our competitors can just as easily live across the ocean as they can down the street.

Third, the increase in the power of new technologies is startling and enormous. Those who can grasp its potential and be first to apply it to a task will gain such a competitive advantage that they may simply eliminate their competition, no matter where they operate in the world or what traditional tasks they have performed in the past.

Fourth, some of our global competitors appear to be much more able to quickly use new technology. Consider the Japanese automobile industry. The use of robotic equipment has allowed Japanese automobile makers to surge to the lead in worldwide sales in just a few short years. Even today, the North American automobile industry lags behind Japan in the use of high-tech equipment that substantially improves car production.

Fifth, the use of new electronic tools has already significantly changed the modern workplace. Technology has greatly altered where people work, when they work, and how they work. In addition, new skills are needed to survive in jobs where those skills were not needed as little as a few years ago.

Sixth, educators have the responsibility of preparing their students for success in the technology-rich world they will face after graduation. Equipping students with appropriate skills, knowledge, and attitudes is critical if we hope to keep schools relevant in the modern world.

We must understand the significance of these points if we hope to compete in the game, whether the game relates to business or education. Mastering change created by technology requires the ability to work with discomfort. As we begin to understand the connection between new technologies and our level of comfort in dealing with them, we must find ways to become more quickly adept with these technologies. We must also understand that other countries and organizations are already able to do this. What is it that they have done that allows them to apply new technologies more readily than others?

What Is the Key to Success?

Does the key to success lie with the technology? Does having more computers, robots, networks, and satellites really make a significant difference? The answer lies less with the technology and more in the mind-set or paradigm of the people who use the technology. Mind-set determines how people visualize the potential of new technology, and mind-set determines the way it is used to enhance our professional and personal lives. If mind-set is driven by a desire for comfort, it can drastically limit even the most powerful new technologies. For far too many of us, this desire for comfort dramatically outweighs our need to push the limits of what new technologies can do.

Clearly, the key to success lies in how we perceive and apply the new technologies. There will be great winners and losers as society moves further into a technology-based world. It is a way of life that we can only begin to imagine. Thus, the key to success in the emerging culture of the 21st century is being able to make a radical shift in our mind-set or paradigm for life.

1

The Power of Paradigm

Paradigm is a model, perspective, value system, frame of reference, filter, or worldview that guides one's actions. Paradigm governs everything we do and everything we think. Our paradigm colors our perception of the world, and it determines the way we see significance in events around us and how we find meaning in our lives. We use our paradigm to set priorities for our personal and professional lives. It is stamped into us as we pass through the early and most impressionable years of our lives.

The power of paradigm to influence our perception cannot be overstated. Following is a simple activity that will help you understand how paradigm can affect perception. As an example, think back to the first time you saw a picture like this.

Can you see the old woman? Can you see the young woman? Look at the separated images in the next image if you are having trouble.

We can both remember becoming completely frustrated when someone said there were two pictures here—that of an older woman and that of a younger woman. Try as we did, we just could not see them both. Then suddenly, and for no apparent reason, our focus shifted and there they both were. Once we understood how to change our focus, it was simple to move back and forth between the two images. In retrospect, it is hard to accept that there was ever a time when we could not see both images. In much the same way, many people have had a similar experience when viewing the 3-dimensional pictures in which you are presented with two side-by-side images to look at. Many people simply cannot see the 3-D image that pops out of the page when each of their eyes focuses on a separate image. Has this ever happened to you?

For those of you that have never seen this illustration before, the two women in the previous picture have been separated for you. Even if you have seen this image before, notice that your mind has to reassess the nose of the old woman as the chin of the young woman as you quickly move your eyes between the two images.

The point here is that once your mind starts seeing images in a certain way, it takes real effort to see them from a different perspective. In fact, you might even call people crazy if they told you they saw something else in a picture you had already begun to see in a certain way. It is amazing how your mind-set can prevent you from seeing the validity of another point of view.

⌐ Paradigm and Real Life

Imagine the mind-set of a farmer in 1908 who relies on horses for transportation. He is in his wagon behind reliable old Bessie, a strong mare with the ability to pull the farmer and his supplies all the way home. On the way to town, both are startled by the sudden appearance of a noisy motor car, chugging along on its own power. As the motor car leaves him choking in its dust, the farmer swears at the folly of this noisy, dirty contraption. If we were to ask him at that moment whether this automobile would have any significant impact on the future, he would not hesitate to share his perspectives— there is absolutely no future for the automobile, he would tell us. There is not enough gasoline around for these cursed horseless carriages, no one knows how to fix them when they break down, and besides, they scare the horses. More important, there is not enough room on the road for both cars and horses. Because building separate roads for motor cars is impractical, it is a certainty that these blasted things will be gone in a year or two.

From our perspective, as we stand well into the future, it is easy to chuckle at his seeming shortsightedness. The reality is that the automobile, and its spin-off technologies, changed everything. In short order, the automobile had an impact on virtually every part of industrialized society. It changed the way we lived, played, and viewed the world, but from where the farmer sat on his wagon behind Bessie, none of this seemed possible or even probable. His mind-set, his paradigm, would not allow him to see change even as it sped by him on the road blowing dust and fumes in his face. He just could not see the future even though it was staring him in the face.

Although we may laugh at such situations, it is highly possible for any one of us to be in a similar situation as this farmer. It is highly possible and probable for any one of us to view a technology and completely miss its true significance. This is because our paradigm is neither ready nor equipped to deal with our current perspectives, particularly when it comes to new technologies.

Here is a real-world application of the concept of getting locked into a mind-set: What does a farmer who has been raised in a world based on horse power think when he sees his first automobile? Will he be able to grasp the significance of what is staring him in the face?

Paradigm Paralysis

Another example of how paradigm can have a major impact on perception is the invention of the digital watch. In an article titled, "Paradigms: The Business of Discovering the Future," Joel Barker (1993) details this remarkable story. The introduction of electronic watches in the 1970s produced one of the most startling shifts in business in the 20th century. Before the digital watch was invented, there was a paradigm for watches. It was an analog device that included gears, springs, levers, jewels, and the need for daily winding. Time was displayed by continuously moving hands. At that time, most of the world's watches were produced in Switzerland. In 1970, the Swiss controlled 85% of the world's production of fine watches. Watches and clocks had looked and worked the same way for literally hundreds of years, and this was a firmly established mind-set. It was this paradigm that all but killed the Swiss watch industry.

When the first digital watch was developed by Swiss scientists in the early 1970s, the response from the Swiss watch industry was fascinating. They carefully considered this new device and noted that it did not have gears, springs, moving parts, jewels, or a need to be wound. Applying their existing paradigm, they dismissed the digital watch by concluding that it really was not a watch. Although it was their very own researchers who had created the new paradigm, the Swiss watchmakers missed the window of opportunity. They just could not see its potential because of their mind-set.

Seeing little value in this new product, they subsequently sold it to Texas Instruments who in turn sold it to Seiko. It was not the Swiss but their Japanese competitors who saw very early on the market potential for the digital watch. So it was the Japanese who brought the digital watch to the world in the mid-1970s, and it was the Japanese who in short order took the world market for watches away from the Swiss. As a result, by 1980, the Japanese produced 33% of the world's watches and controlled more than 65% of the profits from the manufacture of watches. Meanwhile, the Swiss were left holding less than 10% of the market. More than 50,000 of 62,000 Swiss watchmakers lost their jobs in less than 2 years as a direct result of this oversight. This is what can happen when people are caught in paradigm paralysis!

The results of paradigm paralysis can be swift and devastating for those who are unprepared. However, before we judge the Swiss, we should stop for a moment and reflect back on our experience in viewing the picture of the two women. If we initially focused on one of the women, we probably had difficulty seeing the other. We might also have dismissed anyone who said they saw something else in the picture. Our mind-set would have prevented us from perceiving the entire significance of what we viewed.

This may not look like much of a difference to us today, but it represented a huge shift in paradigm for those who were locked into thinking that watches had to have gears and hands that moved to display the time.

With this in mind, it is much easier to appreciate the response of the traditional watchmakers to the new digital watch technology. The new devices were a radical departure from what watches had looked like for a long time. Some simply dismissed the new devices as toys that would have little or no real impact on the industry. Besides, how could they possibly approach the quality and accuracy of fine Swiss watches? Because they were such a radical departure from what had been, it was hard to even consider them as real watches.

By relying on their old paradigms, the Swiss were blind to the true power of the new electronic watch. This was a critical mistake. Within a few short years, the global watch market shifted to the Orient as sales of electronic digital watches overtook and then left behind the now old-fashioned, gear-based analog watches. Swiss watchmakers hardly knew what had hit them. They were unable to compete because their response was significantly compromised by their paradigm.

But There Is Hope

Before we leave our discussion of the Swiss watchmakers, there is something else you should know. As we write this book, the top-selling watch in the world is produced by Swatch—as in *Swiss watch*! The desperation in the Swiss watch industry after the sudden emergence of digital watches led Swiss companies to take drastic steps to avoid the complete collapse of their business. They were forced to quickly adopt a new mind-set to compete in the new business environment. In the same way that Japan and Germany rose from the destruction of the Second World War, the Swiss have resurrected their watch industry with new digital models that have taken the world by storm.

So there is hope for those suffering from paradigm paralysis, and that is good news because the magnitude of change facing everyone in the 21st century will mean that we will all suffer from paradigm paralysis at one time or another. But there is a catch: We have to be willing to take drastic measures to recover.

Paradigm Paralysis in the Classroom

It is easy to think that these types of things happen to someone else somewhere else. However, paradigm paralysis is everywhere! Other examples of the power of paradigm can be found in education. The technology used in today's classrooms is very different from the technology used by students hundreds of years ago, but paradigm paralysis was evident even then. Looking back, it is easy to be amused by reports that came out about the controversies of an earlier time. Following are some paraphrased examples of paradigm paralysis in the classroom from days gone by as researched by Father Stanley Bezuska (told to David Thornburg in 1991) of Boston College:

- At a teachers' conference in 1703, it was reported that students could no longer prepare bark to calculate problems. They depended instead on expensive slates. There was great concern by the teachers of the time over what students would do when the slate was dropped and broken.

- In 1815, it was reported at a principals' meeting that students depended too much on paper. They no longer knew how to write on a slate without getting dust all over themselves. What would happen when they ran out of paper?
- The National Association of Teachers reported in 1907 that students depended too much on ink and no longer knew how to use a knife to sharpen a pencil.
- According to the *Rural American Teacher* in 1928, students depended too much on store-bought ink. They did not know how to make their own. What would happen when they ran out? They would not be able to write until their next trip to the settlement.
- In 1950, it was observed that ballpoint pens would be the ruin of education. Students were using these devices and then just throwing them away. The values of thrift and frugality were being discarded. Businesses and banks would never allow such expensive luxuries, according to the educators of the time.

In retrospect, it is easy to see that these teachers were as short-sighted as the Swiss watchmakers. But that's the point. These were not dull-witted individuals. Nevertheless, they kept tripping over their paradigms. Their perception of the impact of new technology was greatly affected by their consolidated view of the world. They had no context for the innovation that they were contemplating. Embracing the new would have required them to let go of old ideas and experience they had gained through hard work and a significant investment of time. Letting go of the past is one of the most difficult and uncomfortable aspects of dealing with change.

Today, even as this book is being written, there is a great debate in education about the use of calculators and computers for computation and writing, not to mention the proper role of the Internet for e-mail and access to the World Wide Web. The theme of this book is that by paying attention to history, stepping back from our existing paradigms of life, and learning to let go of our old mind-sets of the world, we can learn to embrace and leverage change without being left behind. But if we discover we are suffering from paradigm paralysis, we have to be willing to take drastic measures if we hope to recover.

2

Window 2
Mounting Paradigm Pressure

Today, much of North American society finds itself in a very similar situation to that experienced by the Swiss watchmakers and the educators described in the last chapter. There have been astounding developments in communications, computers, entertainment, household appliances, product design, and manufacturing. These developments present us with enormous challenges to our mind-set as to how life should unfold, and these are challenges with incredibly high stakes. In fact, our personal, professional, and national survival depends on our ability to both understand and modify our paradigms to meet the changes racing toward us.

It is like a chain of dependence. Our continuing viability relies heavily on whether companies and individuals can adapt quickly enough to keep pace with their global competitors. This adaptability depends on our educational institutions being able to provide the training necessary to continually equip people with the relevant skills required for life in the 21st century. This chain of dependence relies on the ability of all the players to upgrade or replace their existing paradigms as and when needed.

Just look around. Incredible advances in technology face us at every turn. How do we gain the necessary perspective to survive? We certainly do not want to find ourselves missing or ignoring significant developments and consequently going the same way as the Swiss watchmakers. The fundamental message here is that we must not only understand and embrace technology but also learn to use it to its fullest potential. The only way to do this is to learn to continuously let go of obsolete technologies and mind-sets.

If we are unable or unwilling to do this, we face the looming prospect of a drastic and rapid downward economic slide into a lower standard of living. This is the inevitable result of being unable to compete with others who have the necessary skills. This issue is so significant that it must be given our full attention if we are to successfully tackle such an enormous challenge.

⌐ The Speed of Change

The difficulty lies in the way we think that life *ought* to unfold. If we have lived most of our impressionable years prior to the emergence of electronic technology, then we will find it difficult to accommodate or even understand new developments. The reason for this lies in the way that technological development has occurred over human history.

In the past, technological development was very slow. Looking back at the development of computational technology, for example, you will see that our ancestors had long periods of time to adapt to new technologies that were not particularly powerful relative to those emerging today.

That began to change more than 100 years ago. People who grew to adulthood before the microcomputer came into its own understood that their grandparents had seen more unbelievable change during their lifetimes than all the generations before them. They had started with horses as a major mode of transportation and lived to see a man walk on the moon.

Still, the rate of change experienced by our grandparents is nothing compared with what we have experienced in our lifetimes, not to mention what is coming. The rate of change that humanity experienced during the 50-year span from 1940 to 1990 will accelerate during the next few years. Many experts suggest that the changes we have experienced during the past five decades will be absolutely dwarfed by the changes we will have to deal with within the next 5 to 10 years of our lives. This is because today's changes hint, and we mean only hint, at a future world that we cannot even begin to imagine.

Standing back from this, people today are living through a most extraordinary period of human history. The overwhelming majority of development in the quantity and power of computational and communications technology has occurred during the past 50 years. Consequently, an unprecedented situation of rapid development is being created in human history.

Maybe you thought you were the only one who felt like this, but the pace of change in modern life has a great many people feeling overwhelmed. Those people who are locked into more traditional ways of doing things are having the most difficulty.

The Way It Was

Previous to these crazy times, advances in technology had first been understood and then implemented by adults, who in due course taught their children how to use them. Now, primarily because change is a constant in their lives, young people seem better able to cope with change by altering their paradigm and embracing the new age of high technology. In times of rapid change, it is the young people who first grasp the potential of new technology. As a result, in many cases, it is now the young generations who are teaching the older generations how to use new technologies, and it is the older generations who are struggling to catch up and keep up.

Young people today live with a substantially different paradigm than that of their parents. They may not be able to articulate the differences, but they know the life they are living is unlike that experienced by those who are older. A major paradigm shift has taken place, creating something much more significant than a generation gap. More important, this has happened in less time than it takes to create a new generation.

From this perspective, we can begin to understand the incredible threat that paradigm paralysis holds over us today. Although young people may be living the new paradigm for life, we must consider who is in control of most of the world that they experience. Who makes the decisions in business, government, and education? This power is wielded by people who, for the most part, are still operating from an old paradigm for how life should unfold. Most of the people in positions of control and power in North America were born before the early 1970s. They passed through their most impressionable years before the explosion of microelectronics into everyday life.

People born before 1970 did not experience an electronic world in their youth. They did not use computers when they were in high school. They did not enroll in Preparations for the Microelectronics World 101 while in university. Their worldview, understanding of society, and perspectives on the structure of things were created in a world radically different from the world of today. The world they experienced was based on an industrial model of thinking. It did not anticipate that they would need to know how to integrate "smart" electronic devices into their lives. It did not teach them how to get and interpret the new visual information, and they did not learn the implications of instantaneous global communication. In short, the life they experienced did not equip them to handle the world we now see unfolding before our eyes.

The seeming paralysis in dealing with these challenges is a direct result of the unparalleled shift in the ways of the world since the explosion of microelectronic technology into life after 1970. We face the prospect that critical decisions are being made by people who do not really understand the full implications of the changes taking place and who do not understand the impact these changes might have on the decisions they are making. The decision makers are resisting change in the same manner that some people resist buying a new coat. The old ideas that shape their worldview wrap around them comfortably. Change would bring unwelcome struggle. This is a toxic recipe for disaster.

3

Window 3
Assessing Your Paradigm

This book is about the changes that lie ahead, but before we can appreciate the implications of the great changes taking place now and those that will surely occur in the future, we must understand how our past has shaped our view of the world. Remember that the key to the future is people, not technology. The key attribute of successful people in the future will be their paradigm for life. It is important for us to identify the paradigm that shapes a person's perceptions.

How do you understand one's paradigm? How can you identify what experiences or perspectives color a person's thoughts? In this exercise, we are not trying to get a comprehensive picture of all aspects of how our thoughts are formed. Instead, we are attempting to focus on the amount of change that we experienced in our youth and the role that technology has played in our lives. This can be done by looking at when and how our younger years relate to the explosion of electronic technology.

Take a few minutes to answer the questions in Figure 3.1. Answer honestly and remember that the questions relate to when you were growing up (before you reached the age of 20).

Figure 3.1. The Great North American Paradigm Quiz

Which of these statements describes your life experience before you reached the age of 20?	Describes my youth	Does not describe my youth
1. I remember when all girls had to wear skirts to school.	☐	☐
2. I remember when bubble gum cost 1¢.	☐	☐
3. I remember when world events were things you read about.	☐	☐
4. I grew up without a microwave oven.	☐	☐
5. My mother was at home when I came home from school.	☐	☐
6. I remember when the Russians were the bad guys.	☐	☐
7. Our household telephone had a rotary dial.	☐	☐
8. I remember the assassination of President Kennedy.	☐	☐
9. I rode in a car that was not equipped with seat belts.	☐	☐
10. I grew up never owning a Sony Walkman or similar device.	☐	☐
11. I remember when smoking was considered acceptable.	☐	☐
12. I remember our family getting our first TV.	☐	☐
13. I remember when "made in Japan" meant cheap imitation junk.	☐	☐
14. I, or people I knew, used a slide rule in school.	☐	☐
15. I remember when encyclopedias were only printed on paper.	☐	☐
16. I never played video games in my youth.	☐	☐
17. I had others type my essays or labs in school/university.	☐	☐
18. I rode in a car with a gas-guzzling V8.	☐	☐
19. I wore low-tech running shoes with canvas uppers and uncushioned rubber soles.	☐	☐
20. I washed dirty dishes by hand.	☐	☐
21. I have no video tapes of my youth.	☐	☐
22. I remember when chocolate bars were 10¢.	☐	☐
23. I had 45 rpm and 33 rpm records.	☐	☐
24. My father/mother worked for one company for 20 years or more.	☐	☐
25. I saw learning as the memorization of facts.	☐	☐
26. I grew up without ever using a telephone answering machine.	☐	☐
27. I remember the first time a man stood on the moon.	☐	☐
28. I never had a bicycle that had at least 10 gear combinations.	☐	☐
29. Growing up, I expected to have one career in my life.	☐	☐

⌐ Analyzing Your Score

If three or fewer of the statements in the paradigm quiz describe your life experience before you reached the age of 20, then you probably experienced a technology-rich environment as you grew up, where change was an ever-present factor to be dealt with. The changes taking place in life today are not likely to be causing you a great deal of mental anguish, but read on. Just because you are having less trouble with the changes we are experiencing now does not mean you are exempt from the effects of change that will happen in the future.

If four to six of these statements describe your youth, then your youth likely began before the new age of technology and extended into it. You have also experienced a relatively technology-rich environment, and you know the effects of increasing change as a common part of life. However, you will probably have more difficulty in adapting to change than those who experienced this environment all their lives.

If seven or more of these statements describe your life experience before you reached the age of 20, then you probably grew up before microelectronic technology exploded into our lives. We expect that the majority of readers of this book will fall into this category. Your experience in life today stems directly from your past. The life you experienced when you were growing up did not prepare you for a world of constant change and increased use of powerful technologies. It is important to understand the implications of the world that shaped your mind-set if you want to know how to prepare for success in the radical new life now emerging as we enter the 21st century.

⌐ It Is Not Just the Older Generation

Putting the worldviews described in the paradigm quiz to work, we begin to understand that everyone has a paradigm. Whether we are 6, 12, 18 years old or older, we all have a set picture of the way we think life should unfold. We also begin to see that all of us, even the youngest of us, must learn the skill of unlearning. To become skilled at changing our paradigms and cultivating the ability to embrace change, we must learn to let go of our old paradigms for how life operates.

However, it is a worldwide phenomenon that there are a huge number of people who grew up in a vastly different world than the one they are now experiencing. If you grew up before the age of high technology, you were prepared for life in the Industrial Age. You expected to live in much the same way your parents and grandparents lived, with ideas and institutions that have existed for hundreds of years. This once-successful approach to life is deeply entrenched in the public consciousness. Some changes and adjustments have happened slowly over time in the Industrial Age, but the basic premise for living has not changed significantly. Because many people reading this book have this as their early life experience, it is important that we take a moment to examine the basic foundations of life in the late Industrial Age.

⌐ The Major Foundations of Industrial Life

The Industrial Age can be described as the age of mass production. This era began 300 years ago with the automation of industrial equipment using steam power. The idea of production on a massive scale was refined when Adam Smith developed the concept of the division of labor. This concept was further refined in the early 20th century by Eli Whitney, Henry Ford, and Frederick Winslow Taylor. Taylor captured the essence of this new approach to production in what he called the principles of scientific management. These principles were used to build modern production facilities that used an assembly line. These developments allowed the production of goods at an unprecedented rate. These ideas had profound and immediate effects on business, education, and people.

Mass production resulted in a society based on standardization. The assembly line approach to production did not allow for much, if any, customization. There was a remarkable "cookie cutter" mentality to business, education, and even personal life. Society stamped out a look and feel for life that was almost identical for all. In the vast majority of cases, the needs and desires of the individual were sacrificed in favor of the perceived average needs and desires of the masses. When asked about custom paint jobs on his cars, Henry Ford once replied, "You can have any color. . . as long as it's black."

This "cookie cutter" mind-set of mass production persists widely in life today. How often have you gone into a shop wanting to get some changes made to a product or service they sell only to be told that it is impossible, will take a long time, or will be very expensive? As a result of that type of mind-set, today we are TTWWADIed (That's the Way We've Always Done It) to death. In fact, even today the attitude of many people in business is a take-it-or-leave-it one that has its roots in the Industrial Age paradigm. This paradigm had those who made things deciding what the people wanted and needed.

Industrial life also gave rise to the age of the specialist. The idea behind the assembly line was that people specialized in a particular part of the production process and focused only on their job, not concerning themselves with the things that happened before or after their particular task. Specialization often meant that individual workers did not have a sense of the whole process. It also meant that people, to be successful, needed the ability to blindly follow instructions. It was a basic foundation for all of industrial life, extending far beyond the production line. How many of you have ever asked a person in a bank, department store, or insurance company for assistance only to be told, "That's not my department!" This kind of specialization and compartmentalization is typical of Industrial Age thinking.

The assembly line approach to breaking tasks down into areas of specialization was applied across all societies in the Industrial Age. How many times have you heard someone say, "That's not my department."

Schools in the Industrial Age were designed to prepare people for work in industrial factories and businesses. The mass production mentality standardized all aspects of education. Students were educated in an assembly line approach where they moved from a teacher who specialized in one particular subject to another teacher who specialized in another subject. The needs and desires of the individual student gave way to the perceived average needs and desires of the masses. In this system, working without a sense of the whole, seeing life as a series of separate parts, and following instructions were highly valued.

Business in the industrial world involved central planning, control from the top down, and a hierarchical structure of management. People working in industrial companies climbed the ladder to success, moving up the organization's hierarchy of management one step at a time. Large amounts of money were needed to build production facilities, so the Industrial Age gave rise to the large corporation. These were companies large enough to have the resources needed to produce, sell, and distribute many items to large markets. These large companies were also able to provide their employees benefits that had never before been offered. By the latter half of the 20th century, employees enjoyed pensions, medical plans, and other benefits that were a direct result of the success of this model.

Industrial life was also amazingly predictable. The assembly lines created by large companies made for lives that were filled with the repetition of making similar products day in and day out over a long period of time. Life followed the same pattern year after year. Frequently, people would be employed by a single company for their entire working careers. However, job satisfaction was typically low. Because of the division of labor and the specialization of tasks, an individual often felt like nothing more than a small cog in a huge process that was completely out of the worker's control. Many times, individuals never understood the whole process of production that they were involved in for their entire careers.

If you grew up in this society, its paradigm has been imprinted on your unconscious mind. More and more, however, this mind-set is out of sync with the world in which we now live. People who continue to operate from the assumption that little, if anything, has changed and continue to think the old ways of doing things still work are having an increasingly difficult time functioning. When confronted with change in their lives and their world, they experience conflict and upheaval. This leads to an increased yearning for life to return to the way it used to be. This is a good news/bad news scenario. The good news is they know something is happening. The bad news is that there will be more struggle and discomfort if they persist in trying to make an Industrial Age paradigm work in the Information Age.

Making adjustments to an industrial paradigm may make our lives relatively more successful, but it will not help us keep up with a future that is zooming ahead at the speed of light. People operating with a new paradigm for the Information Age find themselves much further ahead. Trying to make an industrial mind-set work in today's world is like trying to roll a large boulder up a hill that is getting steeper and steeper. It will get harder and harder to make progress until the hill gets so steep that the boulder cannot be moved at all. Finally, the weight of the boulder will become too much to hold and it will fall back on the person holding it. In the same way, trying to function in the modern Information Age with an Industrial Age mind-set will get harder and harder until it stops working altogether. What is needed is a new mind-set that can leverage the power of the technology of change.

4

Window 4
The Technology of Change

There are *yabbuts* (yeah. . . but—) out there who just cannot understand why the old paradigm of industrial life will not work today and into the future. What has changed so drastically? In a word, technology. Although technology is not and must not be our single focus, we cannot ignore modern technological developments. The growing power of these devices is having unprecedented influence on our society. In fact, technology is driving so much change that, increasingly, we ignore it at our personal and professional peril.

To fully appreciate the impact of technology on modern life, it is important to understand the development of technology throughout history. Consider the development of computational devices. Computational technology is arguably the most powerful and pervasive force in our world today. Each new device that appears has the potential to separately create change, but we cannot just consider each new device in isolation. Many other technologies follow the same dramatic pattern of development and growth in power over time. An understanding of this astonishing pattern can help us better grasp what is now happening as well as help us anticipate how it will affect life in the future.

Let's construct a graph that illustrates the increase in the power of computational devices over human history. We will focus on 10 significant developments in humanity's quest for computing power. Although there are many other developments that could be included on the graph, these 10 developments should give us enough data to understand the bigger picture.

1. Counting stones. Technology has always been the consequence of meeting a need because necessity is the mother of invention. Early computational devices were developed as a response to the new ways of doing things in agricultural life. When people stopped chasing animals and began herding them, there was a need to keep a count of the number of sheep, cattle, or goats in the herd. To meet this need, each morning as the animals were being let out of the pen to graze, the farmers would throw a stone onto a pile to represent each animal. At the end of the day, the farmer would take a stone off the pile for every animal that came back into the pen. This simple memory device was sufficient for meeting the modest computing needs of agricultural life.

2. The abacus. By 460 B.C., commerce had developed to the extent that more complex calculations were required. The abacus was invented to meet that need. In essence, an abacus is little more than an organized pile of stones that allowed the operator to perform calculations as well as store numbers. Although the abacus could be used for complex calculations, the device itself was not particularly powerful because the program for properly using the device was completely in the head of the person using it.

3. The mechanical gear-based calculator. In European society during the 1600s, the need for faster and more accurate calculations had increased. The sheer size of the population made commerce and government considerably more complex. In 1642, the son of a French tax collector decided to apply the technology used in clockwork gears to make a calculating device. Blaise Pascal created the first computational device that actually performed partial calculations outside the human brain. As a person moved the crank on his calculator to add numbers, the arrangement of gears would automatically handle the computations as numbers moved into the tens, hundreds, and thousands. Pascal's device suffered from deficiencies in the metallurgical science of the day because the gears could not be made strong enough to handle very large numbers. Still, the concepts Pascal developed were sound, and gear-based calculators using his ideas were produced right up into the 1970s.

The technology of the time was based on gears, springs, and levers. Pascal used these innovations to design the first device that performed calculations outside the human mind.

4. The electromechanical computational device. The problems of commerce and government continued to get bigger. By 1880, the U.S. census involved almost 50 million people. The specific problem the government faced was in the time it was taking to complete a census. The 1880 census took more than 8 years to complete, and experts predicted that the 1890 census would take 13 years to tabulate. A man named Herman Hollerith responded to this challenge by using electricity to improve the operation of the gear-based calculator. He used electromagnets to move the gears in his device. He also developed an ingenious way to store numbers as holes punched in cards and to read those numbers directly off the cards into the calculator. He used these holes to allow just the right wires to connect and let the electricity flow to just the right electromagnet to move just the right gear. In this way, the machine would count the number of people represented by the holes in the card. His device did the initial tabulation of the 1890 census in just 6 weeks and did the entire evaluation of the census data in 2 years. This device provided the world with its first demonstration of real machine-based calculating power and marked the beginning of the modern era of powerful computational devices. By the way, Hollerith quickly saw the commercial value of his device and left the government shortly after the 1890 census. He formed a company called The Tabulating Machine Company. In 1926, this company changed its name to International Business Machines, which we know today as IBM.

5. Automatic calculation devices. The development of tools of
war was a high priority in the 20th century. The need for calculations for everything from the trajectories of artillery shells to the
development of the atomic bomb required enormous amounts of
complex calculations. Several initiatives were undertaken to improve the power of calculating machines.

In 1937, Howard Aiken started to work on a completely automatic
calculation device that would read the numbers to be used for its calculations, perform the calculations according to a predetermined
program, and print out the results. All this was done without any
intervention by humans. He used telephone relay switch technology
to store the numbers and perform the calculations. This device was
called the Mark I, and when completed in 1944, it became the world's
first fully automatic computer. It could perform a 10-digit multiplication in just 3 seconds. The remarkable computer age had begun.

6. The Electronic Numerical Integrator and Calculator (ENIAC).
Also responding to the great need for calculating power related to
the war effort, Presper Eckert and John Mauchly began working in
1939 on a computer that would be even faster than the Mark I. It
would use vacuum tubes instead of telephone relay switches to
store numbers and perform calculations. Vacuum tubes are
switches that contain no moving parts, rather they rely entirely on
the flow of electrons to operate. This means they are electronic.
This also means they are very fast.

On Valentine's Day in 1946, Eckert and Mauchly began using their
new device known as the ENIAC. It was 1,000 times faster than the
Mark I and could perform a 10-digit multiplication in 3/1000 of a
second. With the development of the ENIAC, the world entered the
Electronic Age.

7. Transistor-based computers. In the 1950s, engineers discovered that using transistors instead of vacuum tubes could make
computers even faster, smaller, and cheaper. A transistor is a solid-
state switching device made (generally) from nearly pure silicon
(a semiconductor), which has been chemically etched and altered
with dopants to form an electronic switch capable of being opened
or closed at incredibly high speeds. They are smaller, faster, cooler,
and cheaper than vacuum tubes.

By 1962, the transistor-based STRETCH computer used by the U.S. Weather Bureau was performing 7 million calculations per second while attempting to simulate weather patterns and project the weather as much as 10 days into the future.

8. Silicon-chip computers. By the mid-1960s, engineers discovered they could make transistors by photographically reducing the diagrams for computer circuitry down to incredibly small chips of silicon to create what was called *integrated circuity.* They were able to produce still faster, smaller, and cheaper computers. Using this technology, large computers in the mid-1970s were reaching speeds of 300 million calculations per second.

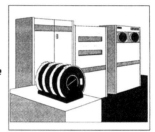

Photographic reduction of circuit patterns onto chips of silicon made it possible to fit an entire computer system in a large room.

9. Microprocessors. In 1969, Ted Hoff, working at the Intel Corporation, reduced all of the circuitry for an entire computer processing unit onto a tiny chip of silicon. This chip was called a *microprocessor.* It single-handedly opened the door for the astounding changes that have taken place in everyday life during the past three decades. The microprocessor was remarkable both for its small size and low cost. Although it was not nearly as fast as the large computers at that time, its power to influence life far exceeded that of any other computational device. It appeared on the market in pocket calculators in 1971 and eventually lead to the development of everything from digital watches to microwave ovens. The microprocessor also led to the development of microcomputers, which first came to the market in assembled form in 1976. The microprocessor has been the single most important development in computational technology to date. The world is still reeling from the impact of this device. Slower than the really big computers, the real power of the microprocessor lies in its incredibly small size and low cost. Today, microprocessors are ubiquitous, in everything from cars and satellites to toasters and birthday cards.

The microprocessor is the single most important development in the amazing story of computing. The proliferation of electronics into the life of the average person was a result of this innovation.

10. Supercomputers. During the 1980s, engineers worked on making microcomputers better and faster. They also worked on astoundingly fast devices called *supercomputers.* Although supercomputers use microprocessor technology, they were (and are) neither small nor cheap. They are, however, blindingly fast. By the 1980s, supercomputers were reaching speeds of more than a billion calculations per second. Today, multiprocessing supercomputers have become unbelievably fast. In 1998, IBM announced it had developed a computer with more than 100 processors that was reaching speeds in excess of 3 trillion calculations per second (no, that's not a misprint).

Now Let's Draw the Graph

Now let's construct our graph of the growth of computational power over time. At least, let's attempt to get an idea of what this graph might look like. As you will see, this is a remarkable exercise. The horizontal axis measures time from the early stages of the agricultural revolution from approximately 8000 B.C. up to the year 2000 A.D. The vertical axis measures the power of the devices. This is a relative measure that considers such factors as the amount of memory, the speed at which it can compute, the functions it can perform, its size, and the cost of the technology.

Let's assume that this graph is drawn on a standard 8½" by 11" piece of paper turned sideways (landscape view). The graph is shown in Figure 4.1. As you can see, the power of computational devices begins a dramatic rise with the development of Hollerith's tabulating machine in 1890. But we have a big problem. If the height of the graph has reached the top edge of the paper by the time we have the power of the Mark I computer in 1944, how do we show the astounding increase in power that has occurred since then? We have to change the scale of the graph because the next device, the ENIAC, was 1,000 times more powerful than the Mark I. That would require a piece of paper 708 feet tall (see Figure 4.2)!

Now let's move on to showing the increase in power in the transistor-based computers. The STRETCH computer in 1962 was performing 7 million calculations per second. To show this increase, we need a piece of paper 2,819 miles high! But wait, we have only just begun. To illustrate the power of computers using integrated circuitry operating at 300 million calculations per second, we would need a piece of paper 120,801 miles high!

The power of microcomputers has proven to be enormous and it would require a piece of paper 805,343 miles high to show just how far computational power has come since we began this development 10,000 years ago. Now hold on to your hats—here is the really astounding part of Figure 4.3: To show the power of current super computers operating at 3 trillion calculations per second, we need a piece of paper that stretches 1,208,013,900 miles into the sky!

So What Does This Tell Us?

Figure 4.3 is a dramatic graph! The astounding height of this piece of paper tells us something very, very big is going on. There are three significant points that can be drawn from this graph: technology development is exponential, the compression of development, and the acceleration of change.

Figure 4.1. The Power of Computational Technology Over Human History

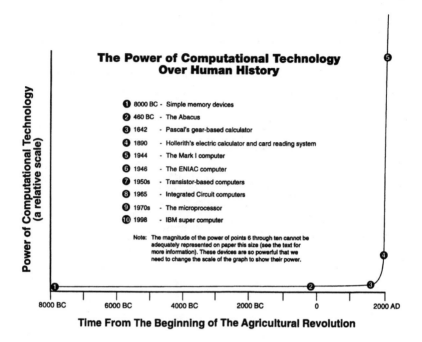

Technology Development Is Exponential

Obviously, the power of technology is increasing remarkably, but there is something even more important to see in Figure 4.1. Not only is the power of technology increasing, but the rate at which it is increasing is growing as well. We are experiencing the effects of exponential growth in the power of computational technology. This means that it is taking less and less time to achieve more and more power. The power of computational devices now gives those who use them such an edge over people who do not use them, that there is really no competition at all. Extrapolating Figure 4.1 into the future, we can predict that people who feel comfortable using new computational technologies will continue to have an incredible advantage over those who do not. With the continuing exponential growth in the power of these devices, no matter how trivial or ineffective they

Figure 4.2. The Increase in Power in Transistor-Based Computers

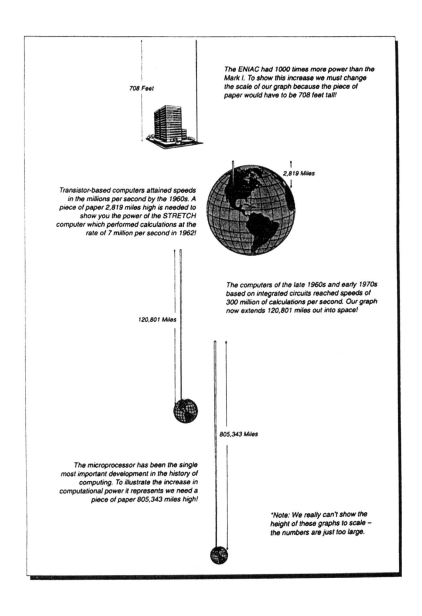

708 Feet

The ENIAC had 1000 times more power than the Mark I. To show this increase we must change the scale of our graph because the piece of paper would have to be 708 feet tall!

2,819 Miles

Transistor-based computers attained speeds in the millions per second by the 1960s. A piece of paper 2,819 miles high is needed to show you the power of the STRETCH computer which performed calculations at the rate of 7 million per second in 1962!

The computers of the late 1960s and early 1970s based on integrated circuits reached speeds of 300 million of calculations per second. Our graph now extends 120,801 miles out into space!

120,801 Miles

805,343 Miles

The microprocessor has been the single most important development in the history of computing. To illustrate the increase in computational power it represents we need a piece of paper 805,343 miles high!

*Note: We really can't show the height of these graphs to scale – the numbers are just too large.

Figure 4.3. The Increase of Computational Power

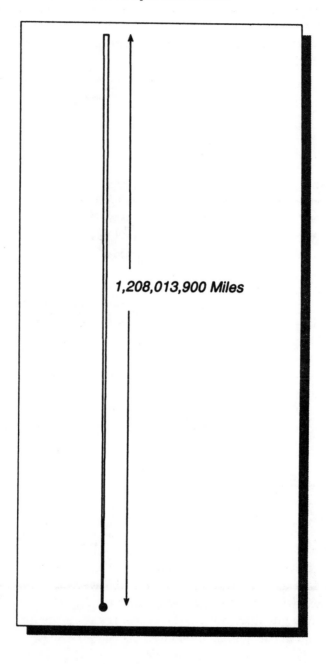

1,208,013,900 Miles

might initially appear, we cannot dismiss them. Any new device cannot be viewed as a single entity. Rather, it must be considered as part of the continuum from where it has come from to where it is going. The fact that continued development is underway on a device or application of technology should be a signal that significant changes will occur in that field in the very near future. Those who choose to ignore these developments are like the proverbial ostrich with its head in the sand.

The Compression of Development

Looking at Figure 4.1, it is important to note that this remarkable development of computational power has been compressed into the past 50 years. The impact of this compression is even more remarkable when we consider that most of the initial work on these technologies was done behind closed doors. Until the introduction of the microprocessor, the average citizen knew very little about developments in computing. The machines were costly and they were kept in locked rooms for purposes of security and cleanliness. The general public was not aware of how far this technology had progressed until microprocessors burst onto the scene in the early 1970s. Most people were first jolted into the electronic computer age more than 25 years after the ENIAC was first turned on. It must be stressed that this was not a minor shift in a peripheral area of life. In the space of 10 years, microprocessors invaded virtually every major human endeavor from entertainment to medicine and everything in between.

The Acceleration of Change

Consider the amount of change that has occurred over time from the perspective of a typical person's life span. Consider any 70-year period in the 10,000 years covered by Figure 4.1. Look at the amount of change in computational technology that took place during that period. Life spans that encompass the past 30 years of history have had to deal with more change than in any other time in recorded history. Simply put, this means that no generation has ever had to face the amount of change as those in the past 30 years have.

Electronics have increased in power
more than 1,000,000 times since the
development of the ENIAC, but the
greatest changes still lie ahead.
Fasten your seat belts!

It is this compression that has resulted in the dramatic and abrupt change in life experience that we have been talking about. People who grew up before these developments were simply not equipped with the concepts and skills needed for success in this new technology-rich world. This was mainly because virtually all of these changes were still unseen at that time. It is easy to understand why some people, growing up before the explosion of electronics, are having a difficult time coming to terms with, let alone catching up to, these changes.

However, Figure 4.1 also gives us a clue as to the nature of the changes that will confront us as we move into the 21st century. This is because the exponential upward swing of the power of computational technology does not stop. Not only will it continue, but the rate of change will also increase. Comprehending the concept of accelerating technological power is absolutely pivotal to grasping what this book is all about. By understanding the rate and the power of the changes coming at us, we can begin to see what must be done to synchronize education with the rest of the world.

5

Moore's Law

As we have just discovered, it is not just that the world is changing, it is that the rate and nature of change is also changing. We can blame this on Moore's Law.

Gordon Moore was the cofounder and chief executive officer for the Intel Corporation, the major force in the creation and production of the microchips that drive most of today's computers. In 1965, a little more than 3 years before Intel was founded, Moore wrote an article for *Electronics* magazine in which he predicted that the power and complexity of the integrated circuits would double every 12 months. He later modified this estimate to 18 months.

What Moore suggested was that the density of electronic components on a chip would double every 18 months while its cost would decrease by 50%. Simply put, Moore's Law states that if you were to take the most powerful computer that exists on earth today, 18 months from now there will be a computer that will have twice the processing power, speed, and capability of that computer. Looking back, we see that the power of a Cray super computer that existed as little as 10 years ago is now available to the average consumer at a local electronics store. In fact, based on Moore's Law, what was a Cray 10 years ago would now be called a Sony PlayStation without color. The relentless drive of Moore's Law has created whole new industries for such products as digital watches, calculators, video games, the Internet, smart phones, digital television, and who knows what else on the horizon.

Moore's Law has proven accurate for more than 30 years. How long will this continue? Moore told *Time* magazine in June 2000 that he believes this remarkable growth will continue for at least another 10 and perhaps as many as 20 years before the laws of atomic structure will slow things down. After that, Moore predicts that doubling will continue, but perhaps at a somewhat slower rate, suggesting that the rate may be every 3 years instead of every 18 months. And remember, he was not even discussing the impact photonics (light-based computers) will have on increasing technological power.

It is time to stand back and consider what such dramatic growth really means. Although this is exceedingly difficult to put into perspective, the implications of Moore's Law spell out dramatic technological developments for the future. It is critical that we grasp the significance of the power of doubling outlined in Moore's Law if we hope to understand what is going to unfold in a very short period of time.

⌐ The Power of Doubling

To illustrate what doubling technological power will look like, let's use an analogy. Imagine you are going to build an addition onto a school. You have responsibility for the project and have just received the bids for the work to be done. Predictably, they are all fairly close to the projected cost of $3 million.

You are just about to break ground for a new addition to a school when you get a surprising offer: The contractor only wants 1¢ for the first day's work, and he will charge you only for one month. What is the catch?

However, the last bid has a remarkable proposal. It comes from a well-respected contractor and it goes like this: The contractor will only charge 1¢ for the first day of work including all materials, equipment, and labor. The only thing he asks is that you double the amount he is paid each day for a month, let's say August. That's it. After a month, he will not charge you another penny, no matter how long it takes to complete the work. Right off the top, this sounds like a great deal, right? Because this proposal comes from a good contractor, you decide to take him up on it. Now let's see how it works out. Your payments start off like this:

Day 1	$.01
Day 2	$.02
Day 3	$.04
Day 4	$.08
Day 5	$.16
Day 6	$.32
Day 7	$.64
Day 8	$1.28
Day 9	$2.56
Day 10	$5.12

After 10 days, your total output has been $10.23. No problem. In fact, this is better than our wildest money saving dreams! Let's continue:

Day 11	$10.24
Day 12	$20.48
Day 13	$40.96
Day 14	$81.92
Day 15	$163.84

Half the month is over and you are laughing all the way to the bank. Your total expenditure is now just $327.67.

Day 16	$327.68
Day 17	$655.36
Day 18	$1,310.72
Day 19	$2,621.44
Day 20	$5,242.88
Day 21	$10,485.76
Day 22	$20,971.52

Day 22 is an important one to ponder. You can see that the contractor is now starting to get a reasonable amount of money for each day, but you have still only paid out a total of $41,943.03. This is still far below the other bids of $3 million. This seems too good to be true, and it is. Watch what happens as the doubling effect really begins to kick in.

Day 23	$41,943.04
Day 24	$83,886.08
Day 25	$167,772.16
Day 26	$335,544.32
Day 27	$671,088.64
Day 28	$1,342,177.28
Day 29	$2,684,354.56
Day 30	$5,368,709.12
Day 31	$10,737,418.24

It's time to call 911.

The total you would end up paying is more than $21 million! Wow! It is important to note that the doubling has the greatest impact in the last few days. (Why didn't you build it in February?) In the beginning, did you really have any idea that starting at 1¢ would lead to such an astonishing amount? The answer for most of us would certainly be no.

However, this is an accurate representation of the power of something that is constantly doubling in value. At first, the change is so slight that its power is deceiving. We can easily be lulled into thinking that nothing much of significance is happening and therefore dismiss it as inconsequential. While we are busy ignoring what is happening, the power of the doubling continues to work relentlessly. In particular, consider the impact the last 3 days has on the total amount. Unfortunately, when we finally become aware that something is going on, it may be too late. The doubling effect has already reached a point where massive changes can occur very quickly.

Now let's relate this example to Moore's Law: Electronic technology has been doubling in power every 18 months for more than 40 years and will continue to do so for quite some time. What does this mean? It means be warned; when it comes to the growth and impact of technological power on our society, we have only reached Day 22, if that! What lies ahead is almost beyond our ability to comprehend. Just like the contractor being paid a wage that doubles each day, the doubling of technological power will have its greatest impact in the last few days of the month. But remember, there is no end to the month in technological development. There is no Day 31. The growth in power will continue into our foreseeable future. So just what does technology have in store for us?

6

Window 6
Looking at the Road Ahead

⌐ Live Life as a Quarterback

The world is undergoing a rate of change that is unprecedented in human history. We need to change just to survive. So how do we anticipate the necessary changes? To develop effective long-range goals in an environment of fast-paced changes, we must begin by looking at life the way a quarterback looks at the football field when he throws the ball.

When a quarterback steps up over the center knowing he is about to start a passing play, he has to become a futurist, anticipating where everyone will be in 3 to 5 seconds. Consider for a moment what goes on inside the quarterback's mind as he takes the snap, drops back, and sets up to throw. The quarterback cannot throw the ball to where the receiver *is* but, rather, to where the receiver is *going to be*. The reason is that he is dealing with a moving target. If the quarterback throws the ball to where the receiver is, by the time it arrives, the receiver will be long gone. To be successful, a quarter-back must live in the future, visualizing the future event and then working his way back to the present to determine what he must do to make that future event happen. It is really about seeing the present as nothing more than the past of the future.

The only way to see properly in times of change is to live life like a quarterback.

Today, we must work in much the same manner in the modern world. The world is no longer the static, predictable place it was during the late Industrial Age. It is now a moving target, one that is picking up speed. To be successful, we must start looking at where the world is *going to be,* not where it *is.* To do this we must all learn to use our intuition. We are not referring to some sort of mystical crystal ball gazing done in a small, darkened room filled with the pungent aroma of burning incense. On the contrary, what we are referring to here is a highly rational process of making reasoned extrapolations based on major trends that are now unfolding. We must consider life through the lens of emerging technologies. When we begin to live our lives this way, we are able to constantly look into the future.

⌐ Looking for Trends

Let's try to get an idea of where the world is heading over the next 10 to 15 years. By putting what we know about change and technology together, we can begin to see what is coming. The following are four major trends in technological development that we simply cannot ignore:

1. Global digital networks
2. Technological fusion
3. Emerging strategic alliances
4. Personal computers for everyone

Trend 1: Global Digital Networks

The remarkable growth in the computer industry during the past 10 years is directly connected to the evolution from big computers to desktop machines. Once the sole domain of large companies and government agencies, desktop computers have become a popular product used almost everywhere. Throughout the late 1980s and into the 1990s, microprocessors have followed Moore's Law, consistently doubling their computing power every 18 months. Today, even the lowliest desktop computers are capable of handling full-motion video, speech-to-text processing, and virtual reality programs. In less than a generation, we have gone from mainframes in a room to mainframes on the desktop! As computers gain the ability to handle new and more sophisticated data, computer users are turning to external data sources. As this dependence on outside information grows, it creates a demand for more sophisticated connections and communication links for both wired and wireless technologies.

This is creating rapid growth in the modem and portable computer markets. Increasingly, companies and government agencies are replacing the desktop computers they purchased in the 1980s and 1990s with those more powerful and portable. This portability makes the workforce more productive while also giving the individual employee the flexibility to work at home, on the road, or in the office.

Another contributing phenomenon has been the tremendous growth of the Internet and World Wide Web during the past few years. This network, which started with four nodes in 1969 as ARPANET (Advanced Research Project Agency), was originally developed for scientists and researchers. It was rumored that the project was sponsored by the Pentagon as part of a protective strategy against nuclear warfare paralyzing the national communications systems. This is false, but the effect of this network has been significant nonetheless. It has taken 30 years for ARPANET to evolve into the global network known as the Internet. Today, the scope of the Internet still provides academics with a way to share their work across vast distances, but it also provides a worldwide mechanism for real-time information, electronic commerce, and entertainment.

In the early 1980s, there were only a few hundred hosts connected to the Internet, but by mid-1999 that number had reached 30 million. At the beginning of 1993, there were very few users of the World Wide Web. This would change quickly because that year a teenager by the name of Marc Andreessen released the first point-and-click graphical user interface for the Internet (Mosaic) and the great explosion in Internet use began. Today, it is estimated that there are between 150 and 200 million individuals and organizations in 123 countries linked to the Internet, with connectivity growing at an average of 10% per month. According to a June 2000 TV ad by Intel, the existing Web continues to expand at a phenomenal pace. According to Intel, in just 24 hours, 2 million new Web pages, 196,000 new Internet-access devices, and 147,000 new Web users will be added. By 2002, it claims that there will be more Web pages than people on the planet. Within a very short period of time, there will be more than a billion Web sites. Some people might interpret this as a trend!

To put this into perspective, the World Wide Web is conservatively doubling in size in terms of content every 100 days. This means that, conservatively, it is increasing in size a staggering 12 times per year! If this continues, more than 80% of the sites that will exist a year from now do not exist today. This is biological growth—like lemmings or bacteria.

Coupled to this is the e-mail explosion. In the United States alone, more than 8 billion messages are sent daily (Qwest advertisement, *Wired,* February 1999). This figure is projected to reach more than 17 billion messages per day in the early part of the millennium. Is it any wonder that e-mail is growing at a thousand times the rate of conventional mail? As a result, telecommunication has evolved from the use of wire-line phones to pagers, fax machines, cellular phones, e-mail, and an amazing array of new devices. Ten years ago, the cellular telephone was marketed as a high-cost service for high-end users, and paging was created to serve specialized users. Today, cellular telephones and paging services are poised to reach mass-market penetration levels of more than 30%. Where will this lead tomorrow?

Collectively, all of these developments are leading to a new mind-set. As little as 3 years ago, cyberspace was primarily for Web jockeys who spent their evenings waxing their modems for greater speed.

Now cyberspace has become a middle-class suburb! This all happened in a world where at the time it still cost you more than $1,500 for the equipment, software, and connections you needed to become jacked in and where downloading files from the World Wide Web was, as described by David Thornburg at the October 1996 Computer Using Educators of California Conference as "like trying to suck peanut butter up a soda straw." Now hold on for just a minute. If we are already having to deal with dramatic changes now, what do you think will happen with the advent of faster lines combined with faster, cheaper, and more powerful computers? Do you think that usage of such devices will increase or decrease?

There can be very little doubt that use will increase dramatically. The speed of technological developments in the telecommunication and computer industries is accelerating at an unprecedented rate, fueled by the popularity of the Internet. This change is affecting the way people do business, creating new products and markets at the foundational level in the process. These changes will fundamentally affect the way we work, play, communicate, and view our fellow citizens. Imagine what effect these events will have on education.

Because these changes are coming more quickly, time between innovations is reduced, which in turn shortens the shelf life of current technologies. As an example, it took approximately 25 years for the one-way pager to become a mass market product, and less than half that time for the cellular phone to become established. It took less than 5 years for the two-way pager to emerge. The world is on a fast track to mobility, that is, the capacity to be anywhere or to place data anywhere. This is a market need that is redefining what and where a business is. The huge demand to be connected anytime, anywhere, and to anyone is driving manufacturers to provide miniaturized, portable communications devices.

The new global digital network consists of ground-based wires and space-based wireless communications.

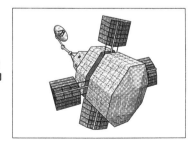

Demographics have a lot to do with the growth of computing and wireless technologies. Although many people from the older generations shy away from the new gadgets and devices, the younger generation is not afraid to work with them. The younger generation is also growing up increasingly comfortable with the use of more electronic data combined with voice. For example, the single biggest market for pagers in Japan is people between the ages of 13 to 20. This suggests that the demographics have less to do with this trend than paradigm.

Growing up in an electronic age has allowed younger people to see the potential of new technologies before their elders. Remember that technology is only technology for those who were born before the gadgets came to the market. We do not refer to automobiles, adding machines, or pianos as technology, and we do not worry about what refrigerators are doing to the nature of food. We just use them. For the cybergeneration, these gadgets and services have always been there. There has never been a time in their lives when they have not had access to television, VCRs, microwaves, Nintendos, and all those other devices that denote their world from ours.

At the same time, the demand for data services has dramatically increased, primarily due to the growth of fax machines, Internet usage, and the emergence of World Wide Web service and content providers. In 1990, 80% of phone transmission was voice. In a September 1999 television ad, the Motorola Corporation said that more than 80% of our wired telephone traffic is data. Worldwide pager and cellular phone subscribers have also been rising steadily in the past few years. According to *USA Today* (1999), in 1988, only 1 of every 100 computers sold was a laptop. In 1998, it was 1 of every 2.2. This trend is a result of businesses becoming increasingly global, which has resulted in an increased number of younger, more mobile professionals who need timely access to information. Such trends led telecommunications officials to predict that within a few years 50% to 80% of all wireless traffic will be data (*USA Today*, 1999).

What happens when more than half of our wired and wireless phone traffic is data transmission? It means that we have a problem. We are quickly overwhelming our telephone system, and this is complicated by the fact that much of today's telephone system is built to handle analog, not digital, traffic. It is not an electronic highway; it is still an electronic dirt road. North American phone service currently relies on more than 160 million miles of copper wiring. As a result, we are still using the POTS (plain old telephone system) for most communications. To bring this system in line with new telecommunication technologies (where the cost of fiber optic cabling is either prohibitive or will take a number of years to install), a new method of moving large amounts of information known as digital subscriber line (DSL) has been developed. DSL is a way of allowing more traffic volume through the existing copper wires that come into our homes, therefore allowing new technologies such as interactive multimedia services into every household. Pervasive change over may take 20 years, but it is coming, and it is safe to suggest that we are rapidly moving toward the electronic highway.

Other innovations, such as coaxial cable and cable modems, will tackle another big problem: two-way information through our television sets. When these technologies become viable, we will be able to access information thousands of times faster than we now can using the Internet. Think about what that might look like. In 1997, we could download 1 trillion bits per second through a single glass fiber with 25,000 gigahertz of bandwidth. That is an astonishing amount of information! According to a Qwest advertisement in *Wired* magazine (September 1999), that is like moving 200 CD-ROMs per second, or all of the text, images, sounds, and video contained in 10 large city libraries from New York to Los Angeles in .0043 of a second. Imagine being able to move information such as this instantly to anyone, anywhere in the world. In the near future, the electronic superhighway will include high-speed fiber cables and wireless and satellite technologies. Satellite technologies could include a global grid of geostationary or low-Earth orbit satellites set in place to keep all of us in touch, all of the time.

This is just the beginning. The Lucent Bell Labs in New Jersey has recently announced that they have reached the 5 trillion bits per second mark down a single glass fiber. A speed of 5 terabits per second is equivalent to sending all the information on 1,000 CDs down a fiber in a single second. Do you think that is fast? Massachusetts-based futurist George Gilder, in a September 1998 speech in San Francisco, to Silicon Valley CEOs, has proposed a parallel to Moore's Law called the Law of the Photon. This law suggests that for the foreseeable future, bandwidth speed will continue tripling every 12 months, while the amount of bandwidth that can be purchased per dollar will double every 18 months. He projects that this increase in bandwidth capacity will continue for at least 20 years. If so, this means that 20 years from now we could be dealing with bandwidth speeds of up to 1 billion times faster than the speeds that are now possible. If this is the case, as hard as it may be to accept, we are literally in the early Stone Age of optical communications. Before we know it, and certainly sooner than we think, a single interactive information network using seamless, high-speed, and global technologies will link our telephones, computers, pagers, televisions, and a myriad of new devices with cable and satellite hookups. Everyone and everything will be connected to everyone and everything else.

The idea of being linked to everyone all the time is mind boggling all by itself. But when we take this trend and combine it with the other three trends shaping our society, we begin to understand why our concept of reality is about to fundamentally change.

Trend 2: Technological Fusion

The development of a global network is creating another trend that involves the blending or convergence of technologies, including voice, data, computing, and communications. We call this trend *technological fusion*. When two or more of these technologies converge and blend, they create technological hybrids whose power is greater than the total power of the individual technologies themselves.

To understand how this is happening, let's consider five technologies and how they are blending together. In 1970, computers, telecommunications, photography, publishing, and television were separate technologies. We could think of them as five circles, completely distinct and different from one another. We have illustrated this for you in Figure 6.1.

By the mid-1990s, these circles had begun moving closer together. Now they are beginning to completely overlap. For example, digital computer photography fuses together computers and cameras, leading to a new technology: the filmless camera. The two circles that have overlapped here are computers and photography. Now other technologies become involved. An example is the development of new cameras that are equipped with cellular modems. This development means pictures can be shot, bounced off satellites, and sent to a different point on the globe—all within seconds of being taken.

These circles now overlap in several different ways (see Figure 6.2). When we step back, we begin to understand that they are rap-

Figure 6.1. Computers, Photography, Publishing, Television, and Telecommunications as Separate Technologies—1970

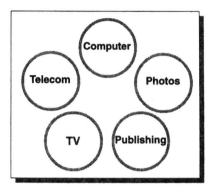

idly becoming one powerful circle, fused together to create a new digital reality: multimedia. This new reality will allow us to capture, process, combine, and communicate all forms of information in any flavor or form we want, including text, video, graphics, or audio (see Figure 6.3).

As this trend progresses, our use of the word *multimedia* will fade away because the real way to describe this use of technology is *monomedia*. It is all just a bunch of digital zeros that can be assembled according to need. When we become comfortable with the concept of monomedia, we will truly be living in a technologically fused world.

In a world of technological fusion, people will watch television through their eyeglasses. They will use virtual reality to do research with a belt clip computer and head-mounted display. Virtual reality will allow doctors to perform remote surgery using robots. It also will allow architects to design and render homes and walk through these homes using computer images before they are built, allowing them to change the details on their designs as they go without ever having to take their project back to the drafting table.

Airplane designers will fly their projects in simulators long before they are ever manufactured, and these simulations are already so real that even today, sometimes pilots cannot tell the difference. Technologies such as this will increasingly become powerful teaching tools. For example, the flight approaches to Singapore recently changed with alterations to that airport. Using fused virtual reality

Figure 6.2. Computers, Photography, Publishing, Television, and
Telecommunications—Today

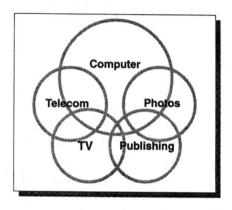

Figure 6.3. Computers, Photography, Publishing, Television, and
Telecommunications in the Future

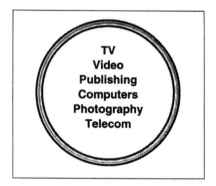

simulation technology, pilots were able to learn the differences without jeopardizing a plane full of people.

Fused hybrid technologies will allow us to do, see, and feel things that were never before possible. Imagine being able to walk inside a calculus function or even to enter the nucleus of an atom. At a certain point, the boundaries between reality and virtual reality will collapse because of the increased sophistication and transparency of these powerful, fused technologies.

Technological Overdrive

According to an F16 pilot we interviewed at Fairchild Air Force Base, during the Gulf War, pilots were equipped with visors that used computers, lasers, and infrared systems. These visors monitored a pilot's eye movements for more efficient laser targeting. A pilot simply looked at the target, and the computer did the rest, firing directly at the target locked in via eye contact.

This same technology is now being used to help people learn. By wearing visors that monitor eye movements, the cognition levels of students can be gauged. The computer can analyze the way students best learn and use this information to help them significantly increase their reading comprehension. This technology, which is based on monitoring eye movements using infrared lasers and computers, is called *hypermation*. As reported in *Wired* magazine in December 1999, there are several publishing companies working on this technology. As the use of hypermated technologies becomes widespread, we will experience a profound revolution in learning.

The use of eye-monitoring technology, such as that used for aircraft control and targeting, will have major implications in the near future.

Furthermore, when technological fusion allows us to carry personal, powerful, tiny, portable, wireless computer systems, our concept of data input will change. In the North American labor market of the late 1990s, 20% of all paid hours and more than 40% of workers were involved in data input. Technological fusion is bringing about changes such as electronic pen-based input and voiceprints. As these technologies evolve, much of the traditional data input work will disappear.

Many hardware and software designers have been working on voice recognition systems and plan to include this technology with all of their new computers. According to Willard Daggett in a March 1998 speech for the Northwest Council of Computer Educators, there are also plans to add voice recognition to the phone system. Automated interpreted telephony would allow the user to speak English into a device to a client in Japan and have their words automatically translated to Japanese. Although this technology is still in its infancy, remember the implications of Moore's Law: The power of this technology is doubling every 18 months. With this in mind, it is easy to see that it will be only a matter of time before technologies such as this become a part of our daily reality.

The amazing synergy being generated by the developing global network and the convergence of technologies is creating more change faster than ever before. As interconnecting technologies become more powerful, they facilitate global access to new forms of information and create new avenues of interpersonal communication.

The two trends of global digital networks and technological fusion are combining to create a new mind-set for what computers are and what they can do. We have moved away from computers as stand-alone devices that work in isolation to technological synergy—global networks form a wired system that allows this to happen. This new paradigm, which is created by these two trends, is working together with a third trend known as emerging strategic alliances.

Trend 3: Emerging Strategic Alliances

There are some very strange bedfellows making headlines in communications, business, and technology news these days. We wonder, and rightly so, what is going on. What is a company such as Sony doing working with Disney? Why are companies such as SEGA, Nintendo, AT&T, Sprint, Paramount Pictures, France Telecom, and Japan NTT joining forces? Why does Microsoft appear to be heavily buying into cable and aerospace technology? And what about the WorldCom acquisition of communications giants MCI and Sprint, or the AOL acquisition of Time Warner/CNN?

The connections here are not immediately clear, although it seems all this is somehow linked to communications systems. It is only when we realize that it is not about phones but about data that we begin to see the attraction of strategic alliances. These companies are looking over the horizon and getting ready for what is coming in the very near future. They see that global digital networks and tech-

The people involved in these new strategic alliances are applying "over the horizon" thinking as they look at the emerging technologies and communications infrastructure. It may not be a complete reality today, but they see enough to tell them that they need to get ready for what lies ahead.

nological fusion will lead us to a whole new world of interactive services.

For example, several years ago SEGA joined forces with TCI, a cable company, and AT&T to offer subscribers the SEGA channel. SEGA and TCI formed an alliance to allow viewers to download video games from satellites via their cable connections. A problem with the technology led them to turn to AT&T for help. The problem was two-way communication. AT&T developed a new cartridge for SEGA called the EDGE, which could plug into the POTS. This allowed the user to connect with others (from AT&T's perspective, preferably as far apart as possible) to play interactive games over telephone lines while keeping a voice channel open so users could talk with each other as they played. New ways of delivering information and interactive services was the goal, and companies around the world began to realize that they must strike alliances to create these new products.

Meanwhile, companies know that their best customers are the ones who can change their mind-sets quickly. SEGA is a prime example of a company targeting young people and doing extremely well because of their marketing strategy. This company sold nearly 9 million units between Thanksgiving and Christmas in 1998 (*USA Today*, 1999). We need to pay attention to the fact that what is happening with real computing is being targeted and marketed to young people. If we are not careful and tuned in to this trend, we will be passed by.

If downloading video games through our cable connections and playing games with people on our POTS is a portent of things to come, what comes next? There will certainly be a wide range of new interactive services that we can only begin to imagine. Already, powerful and versatile prototypes for such devices are being developed and marketed. The TelecomputerTV, a telephone-computer-television device that has recently hit the market, is but one example.

Other interactive services involving television, movies, video games, mail, telephone, banking, and virtual shopping are also being developed. This includes personalized news services that connect newspapers, cable companies, and satellite technology. This personalized news allows the subscribers to choose exactly what they want and only be charged only for what they select.

Consider the trends we have discussed so far. Global digital networks are creating new highways for information. Technological fusion is creating powerful new vehicles to allow us to navigate on these highways. Emerging strategic alliances are creating dazzling new interactive global destinations to visit on the new highways. The fourth development ties these trends together and completes this amazing picture of our future.

Trend 4: Personal Computers for Everyone

Anyone who thinks that a computer consists of a screen, disk drive, and keyboard is stuck in an old paradigm. Computers are no longer restricted to a single form. For example, with a cellular modem and a piece of software called NetHopper, we can cruise the Internet from virtually any point on Earth. The latest Nokia cellular phone is actually much more than that. It is a palmtop device with e-mail, as well as Web, paging, and fax capability. It is neither a phone nor a computer, it is a celleputer.

The Hitachi PC Wallet personal intelligent communicator is on its way to a store near you (Intel advertisement in *Wired*, February 1998). This device contains a powerful microprocessor chip that will allow you to send and receive data, use voice and video for two-way conversation, make presentations, and deliver interactive video teleconferencing. Undoubtedly expensive in the beginning, within months of its appearance on store shelves, you can be guaranteed that there will be dozens of clones at a price point measured in hundreds rather than thousands of dollars. It is important that we understand, however, that this product is not being aimed at older people such as us. Rather, the focus is directly on young people, because increasingly that is where the market is.

As computers become compact, portable, and affordable, fused technology will become available to everyone in the same way that pagers and cellular phones have already become commonplace in a very short time. Most people will have their own particular version of a personal telecomputer or celleputer based on their specific needs. Technology will be for the many, not for the few, as the trend toward smaller, cheaper, and more powerful personal digital assistants (PDAs) unfolds. In the near future, the pocket, wrist, or palm-top computer will become commonplace.

Imagine a world where a global network of telephones, televisions, cables, satellites, and computers connects everyone to everything all the time. Combine this global connectedness with anytime, anywhere, anyhow communication, add the pocket-sized personal technology of the PDA, and you have a recipe for a revolution in the way we think, work, and go about our daily lives.

The impact this will have on virtually every aspect of our existence can hardly be overstated. PDAs will change forever the way we do things. What is emerging right before our very eyes is on a par with the kinds of change created by developments such as the Gutenberg printing press, the harnessing of electricity, the automobile, the telephone, or television.

This global revolution will fundamentally alter the way we work. We are standing at the threshold of a new world—a world in which we will no longer have to be where the work is; it will come to us wherever we are. In this world, people will work with their brains instead of their hands. Communication technologies will create even more global competition, not just for running shoes and laptops but for just about anything we can and cannot imagine. It will, indeed, be a new world. A world in which innovation will be more important than mass production. A world in which investment buys new concepts or the means to create them rather than new machines. A world in which rapid change will continue to be the constant. A world in which workers will compete for jobs with people (and computers) who are not just down the block or across town but around the world. A world at least as different from the one most of us grew up in as the Industrial Age was from its agricultural predecessor.

7

Window 7
It Is Time for Education to Catch Up

This Message Is for Everyone

Education is the foundation of our society. We must understand that any society that relies on a highly complex technological infrastructure that includes highways, railways, airlines, electrical grids, telephones, networks, satellites, and innumerable other high-technology items needs highly competent people to sustain, manage, and develop that society. In the high-technology global market, a nation's ability to compete rests solely on the skill and dedication of its citizens. Many other factors also determine a country's success in the global arena, but if skills and dedication are missing, the rest is insignificant. When these elements are present, they can overcome shortcomings in other areas. So whether we are in business, education, or government, or whether we are retired, we must all see that education is the key to the future. It's everybody's business.

Yes, we mean you! Education is everyone's business, and this has never been more true than in the modern technological world in which an educated workforce is the key to the economic success of businesses and nations.

⌐ How Will the Technology Revolution Affect Education?

Education cannot and will not be exempt from the trends we outlined in Chapter 6. The globalization of information, technological fusion, new strategic alliances, and personal computing power for the masses will transform learning and education in much the same way as it is transforming the way we work and play.

Because we can connect to any information whenever we need it, the concept of time as it is structured in schools is forever changed. The ability to learn wherever we are and whenever we need to means distance is no longer a barrier to learning. For the first time in the history of education, the teacher, student, and content do not need to be in the same place or even be together at the same time. If time and distance are dead and if complete interactive technology allows us to have 2-dimensional and 3-dimensional experiences, what will be left of our current education system?

This is an extremely difficult question. In the face of this unbelievable technological upheaval, it is understandable that educators are struggling for answers. Educational institutions know that they must find solutions to this technology dilemma if they are to stay competitive. Still, workable solutions seem elusive.

If we can accept the premise that we have been caught with our paradigms down, we will begin to see that part of the solution lies in changing these paradigms and creating new schools and new education structures for the millennium that not only understand but capitalize on the four trends discussed in Chapter 6.

Increasingly, we live in a world where change has become the norm. However, many of us grew up in a time where stability was the rule. As we mentioned earlier, *change* as we knew it then was something very different and subtle, and you could measure it in terms of years or even decades. Like children growing up, these changes came on us so gradually that we did not notice them until they were in front of us as measured against last year's growth. Life just is not like that anymore. The doubling of technological power through the 1990s morphed us into a high-speed, high-tech society. As a result, we are all experiencing accelerated change at a pace never before experienced in human history. Most of us involved in education are simply unprepared for this, and consequently, we have not been able to respond to it as quickly as the world outside of education has.

We must quickly catch up or face the unenviable prospect of becoming irrelevant. The key to staying relevant is being able to change our focus. As we have discussed, however, to do this we must understand that our attention cannot and must not be placed on the technology itself. Rather, it must be placed on the mind-set that guides the use of the new technology coming into schools. Thus, shifting paradigms is paramount. We cannot afford to be caught in the backwash as technology races past us; but caught and stuck we are. How could this have happened? Are we truly caught in paradigm paralysis?

Education as a Train

Before we answer this question, let us first picture education as a train. It is pulled by an engine fueled by our desire to educate our children to become effective citizens and to teach them practical skills for success in the world of work. To do this, education must pull many cars down the track—reading, writing, mathematics, geography, history, government, law, languages, science, art, music, woodworking, mechanics, metalworking, and physical education to name a few. Today's schools have even more cars attached to the train in the form of new and different expectations from the public of the school system as modern society continues to change.

Now we are being asked to integrate students with special needs as well as those whose first language is not English. We have become social workers, providing counseling and shelter for students with drug problems or teenage pregnancies. We are asked to watch over those who are victims of physical, emotional, or sexual abuse. We are also asked to take on the role of surrogate parents as families break down. We are expected to build self-esteem, providing personal and moral guidance. All this while being responsible for the delivery of a relevant and meaningful academic curriculum. Despite the many obstacles of money, mind-set, and time, we are pulling the educational train down the tracks faster and more efficiently than ever before, adding new cars as we go. The truth is that educators today are doing a better job than ever before.

Consider education as a train that followed the tracks laid down in the curriculum and was driven by the desires of parents, teachers, and administrators. This train traveled the same tracks for many years with little change in the stable world of the Industrial Age.

⌐ So What Is the Problem?

Consider the impact that technology has had on modern life. Technology has fundamentally and irrevocably changed life for virtually every person in our society. It has compressed time and distance to the point where we can now see history as it happens. World events are viewed as televised miniseries. Consider the Gulf War. We could almost participate with the pilots as they flew their missions over Iraq. We watched Scud missiles blast into Tel Aviv in real time; we saw live interviews conducted with people who were literally halfway around the world. These are but a few indicators of the fact that we now live in an environment with smart, embedded technology: Microwaves come with microprocessors that enable them to perform "smart functions"; wristwatches are also calculators, channel changers, and address books; cars are equipped with microprocessors that tell us that doors are ajar, we need to turn left, or we are low on fuel. Wherever we look, technology is becoming pervasive, embedded, and increasingly intelligent. As a result, many parts of life are being touched, covering everything from recreational activities to the world of work.

Now consider education in this new high-tech environment. Despite our best efforts, education is increasingly disconnected from the rest of the world we just described. Public education has had very little real competition, and as a result, it has become a virtual monopoly. This has dulled many educators to the need to respond to the changes taking place in the outside world. We have responded to many of the dramatic changes in our society, but we have done so from a primarily "educentric" point of view, tinkering with the existing system rather than addressing the four trends discussed in Chapter 6. In other words, schools have opted for trying harder with what *is* rather than working smarter with the new technology and dealing with the changes being forced on the rest of society.

Do you want proof? Compare a classroom in a school to a modern office. Imagine a group of workers who retired 15 years ago returning to their office. What has changed in those years? Everything! Fax machines, personal computers, telecommunications, cellular telephones, voice mail systems, color photocopiers, courier services, the World Wide Web, e-mail telecommuting, video conferencing, and even the systems and ways of doing business—the list is endless. Businesses have had to invent and reinvent themselves again and again during the course of the past 15 years just to survive. Almost nothing from the old office remains except for, perhaps, the watercooler.

Now take those same retired workers back to the schools they attended 40 years earlier and consider what has changed. Although the cultural and social environment of today's schools may have changed significantly, from a structural and instructional point of view, very little, if anything, has changed. We still operate in basically the same school day, same school year, same organizational structure, and same instructional delivery model that was used 40 years ago. How can this possibly be?

This is an important question, and the answer reveals much about the nature of the education system. Before we suggest why these retired workers feel so disoriented at work and so comfortable at school, let's summarize what we have said about the nature of modern life. The message has been clear from the outset of the book: Change has become an integral part of our lives. There is no question that this is disconcerting for the majority of the population. Anyone older than the age of 30 grew up in a much different world from the one that exists today. During the course of the past two decades, we have moved from the late Industrial Age of stability to the Information and Communication Age of constant and even accelerating change. It is not just about change today and status quo tomorrow—it is about change today, change tomorrow, and change forever.

The education system is possibly the most stable institution created by late Industrial Age society. Furthermore, those inside the system have an educentric view of the world that shields them from dealing with it. This sets the stage for a remarkable drama playing out in our schools today. Now consider why our retired workers find their schools so familiar.

Education's Response

How has education responded to this dramatically new techno-logical world we have discussed? The response has come from the educentric perspective. We have not let the dramatic changes out-side education upset the stability of the system. Returning to our train metaphor, we have just added another car called *technology* to an already lengthy train. We have put technologically driven change in a compartment so that traditional instructional activities can con-tinue untouched. Although outside of education, technology has profoundly affected most of the world we live in, the technology car has not had a parallel effect on any of the other cars on the education train. In many schools today, the use of technology is still considered to be little more than just another add-on. It is not seen as a funda-mental and integral aspect of the education train.

So although it is true that this train is improving (and has even added a modern technology car), it is still a train. It is still basically unaffected by the technological developments of modern life. Unlike the rest of the world, where the power of smart devices is changing the rules of life daily everywhere, education has demon-strated an amazing stability and resistance to such change. Our retired workers immediately recognize that their schools have not changed much at all, even after such a long time.

Why? Because many of the people inside the educational system suffer from paradigm paralysis. Like those people we discussed in Chapter 1, educators today are victims of their established mind-sets. This is certainly not to say that they are not intelligent, but rather it is to say that they work in a system increasingly discon-nected from the rest of the world. Worse, there is little if any pressure to connect, let alone keep up, with the rest of the world.

This is because much of the evaluation that takes place in the school system is inwardly focused, where educators compare themselves with other educators. Such a perspective promotes the misconception that we are doing the right kind of work with students. This is the real problem facing education today. We are doing a really good job of providing education, but the kind of education we provide is increasingly irrelevant to the modern changing world in which we live—a world driven by four trends: global digital networks, technological fusion, emerging strategic alliances, and access to personal computers for everyone.

To complicate things, this situation is going to get much worse before it gets any better. Some of our colleagues avoid dealing with the technology issues, thinking that it is just another passing fad. Convinced that this is just like the open classroom, TQM, or outcome-based education, these colleagues believe that this too shall pass. Others quietly remind themselves that they only have 2 years, 5 months, 4 days, and 6 hours to endure until they retire, so why bother? In so doing, many educators are choosing not to recognize the profound shifts that are occurring. The shift from the Industrial Age to the Information Age is upon us. If they ignore it, they run the risk of being left behind in the dust.

If education is a train, with technology in a separate car, the tracks it runs on are Industrial Age thinking. When microelectronics emerged in the late 1970s, the rest of the world left the track that education was on and took a different path. When technological power continued to increase at a truly astonishing rate in the 1980s, the rest of the world got into an airplane because a train simply could not go as fast or change direction as quickly as one that operates in the freedom of the air.

In the 1980s, the world left the train behind and got into an airplane, riding the power of new microelectronic technology.

New dimensions, speeds, and directions were being developed outside of education, but education stayed on its Industrial Age tracks and missed both of these important changes. It continued down the same old track, thinking that it was doing enough by improving the efficiency of the train. The net result was that education became better and better at what it was doing, but at the same time, it became more and more disconnected from and irrelevant to what was happening outside of education.

We must realize that the education system cannot continue operating this way. It cannot continue to get better at delivering an obsolete education. No matter how much the train is improved, it is still a train. The rest of the world has changed. We must also change if public education is to survive. If we choose to ignore this, we will face a train wreck of catastrophic proportions.

⌐ The World in a Rocket

Now we face an even greater challenge. Within the next few years, the world outside of education will be climbing into a rocket and heading for orbit using the new technological devices and powers that are starting to appear in the new millennium. Why a rocket? And why so quickly? Didn't the world just switch from a train to an airplane?

Riding the wave of the dramatic acceleration of technological power of the 1990s, the world is entering a rocket.

The answer lies with the four trends we discussed earlier. Many educators do not yet fully appreciate that the technology they see and use is just part of a continuum of developing technological power. While we were busy with the details of our normal lives, electronic technology steadily doubled in power time and again during the past 50 years.

This doubling process began with the first electronic computer, which became operational in 1944. The microcomputers that appeared in the late 1970s were just one more step in this process. We now see that the new electronic devices have begun to show some real power. This is most certainly affecting our lives. Personal computers, fax machines, smart microwaves, multifunctional wristwatches, cellular telephones, pagers, robotic assembly lines, automated banking machines, and personal portable stereo equipment are just a few examples of devices that have already altered the way we go about our daily lives.

However, the real story is what lies ahead. As the saying goes, "You ain't seen nothin' yet!" The doubling in technological power is about to kick into overdrive in much the same way it did for the building contractor on Day 22. For the contractor, the result was an unbelievable payday at the end of the month. For us, the result will be some truly unbelievable technologies. None of us are prepared for what is about to unfold, and unlike the situation with the contractor, the doubling effect of technological power will not stop at the end of the month. This story of developing technological power will extend well into the 21st century. The day that technology stops doubling has not yet been foreseen. We are about to get into a rocket, technologically speaking.

What will this doubling effect have on our lives? Although it is difficult to accurately predict exactly what the technology will look like, there is little doubt that it will revolutionize virtually every aspect of human endeavor. What about education? Consider the children who are entering the school system in kindergarten right now. What kind of world will they graduate into? What should the school system be doing now to prepare them for that future? With changes of such enormous magnitude coming in such a short time frame, we cannot continue to just tinker with a train that needs a complete overhaul. In fact, it may be time to discard the train. This is because fundamental and pervasive changes are required if we want education to survive, let alone be relevant in the world of the 21st century.

Many educators know that something big is happening today in the world outside of education. Many even say they want a new system to meet the changing needs of the students who will live in the world of tomorrow. Still, they continue to act in the same way that they have for years. Thus their words are just rhetoric, and rhetoric is not the language of change. In and of itself, it cannot transform education.

If a new system is what is needed, we must begin to do things differently. The changes we must make to the way we prepare students for the rest of their lives must be substantial. True, we will not be able 80 to make these changes overnight, but change we must. These changes will take some time, so we need to get moving today. If education hopes to meet the challenge of preparing the students of today for the world of tomorrow, it must break out of its current mind-set and move ahead rapidly to embrace the new paradigm of constant and accelerating change.

8

Window 8
Education in the Future

As that well-known American philosopher Yogi Berra once said, "If you don't know where you're going, you'll probably end up somewhere else." The key to successful change is knowing where we are going. Without a clear goal in mind, much effort may be wasted in heading in the wrong direction. The first thing we must do is establish a goal or target to aim for.

How do we determine what our goal should be, particularly in light of the rapidly changing modern world? To begin, there is a basic rule to follow: We should never limit our focus by looking only at what is "hot" today. We cannot base our decisions just on what exists; rather, as we have discussed, what exists today can only be fully understood when seen as part of a continuum that stretches into the future. For example, if you look at the latest electronic devices and make decisions based just on what you see, you may be very surprised at what happens in the very near future. According to an article in *Business Week* (1998), electronic products in Japan currently have a shelf life of 90 days or so before they are superseded by some new and improved product. The world of technology is changing so quickly that many companies have adopted a corporate motto that says, "Today let's put ourselves out of business, because if we don't, someone else will!" The only way to adequately plan for the future is to look at the big picture that started in the past and move through the present and into the future.

So we must look at education the same way that the quarterback looks at the football field. We must perceive where things are headed so we can respond appropriately. This will require us to apply all that we have discussed in this book. We must accept that we have a paradigm for how we expect life to unfold, and we must accept that in times of radical change, we all suffer from some degree of para-digm paralysis. We must also accept that change requires us to let go of ideas and ways of doing things that we hold dear. Keep this in mind as we now begin to project what education will look like in the future.

Education Will Not Be Confined to a Single Place

For the past 150 years, students have gone to school. However, this is not the way it will always be. This may come as a real shock to many of our colleagues who have spent most of their careers teach-ing in a classroom. The development of a global digital network of fiber-optic cable and wireless communications using satellites and cellular telephones will fundamentally revolutionize the concept of travel. Literally anyone will be able to access this network from any-where using personal, pocket, wireless, tiny-tech communication devices. We are already seeing the first signs of this today.

But why will this have such a dramatic effect on where students learn? First, all forms of information and communication are being converted to a digital format. Television signals, telephone commu-nications, fax signals, and radio transmissions are all going digital. Second, the worldwide network is rapidly blanketing the globe. There are at least four projects currently being developed to place satellite systems in a global grid around the world to provide voice and/or data access anywhere on earth. Third, computers and cellu-lar telephones are being miniaturized. We already have palmtop computers and cellular telephones that fold up and fit comfortably in our pocket.

This is just the beginning. It has been said that AT&T has patents out for cellular telephones that will fit in your ring, your watch, the

Powerful, portable, personal
technology connected to
multimedia instructional resources
via a global digital network means
that a lot of traditional ideas about
education are going to be
challenged.

rims of glasses, a tooth, your cuff links, even an earring. What's next? There is no technical reason why we could not build a nasal implant telephone. Video and digital cameras have been reduced to the size of a pea and will continue to shrink in size. Computers will also continue to shrink from the current palmtop size down to unimaginably small dimensions, only limited by the size of our fingers and our imagination. Put all of these developments together and you can see that the Dick Tracy wristwatch communicator is just around the corner. But the real one will add supercomputing power and a worldwide network that can be accessed from anywhere to the two-way interactive video we have always marveled at in the comics. The impact of the widespread use of this kind of device simply cannot be ignored.

Due to the emergence of these new technologies, learning will not need to be confined to a single place or single source. Students will be able to remain in contact with their teacher and classmates while on vacation, while traveling with a parent on a business trip, or while their parents are working at some remote location. Learning will happen at home, on the job, or in the community. When learners can use the kind of powerful personal computer communicators that will be available in the next few years, learning will literally occur wherever the learner is at any particular moment.

Education Will Not Be Confined to a Specific Time

Personal computer communication devices will also break the time barrier for learning. School will no longer be over when the bell rings at the end of a period or school day. The school day and school year will no longer be predicated on the 5½-hour day, 180 days a year that is a remnant of a time when children were needed in the fields during the summer to help harvest the crops. Using the new technologies, students will be able to access learning materials 24 hours a day, 365 days a year. This will have a major impact on learning because it can be primarily driven by need and/or interest.

Occupational futurists tell us that our children can anticipate that in their lifetimes, they will have 10 to 14 distinct careers—not 10 to 14 jobs working for the same company but 10 to 14 careers. How many of us had parents who worked for the same company or in the same business for 20 or more years? Increasingly, the message that we get from business is that if you want loyalty, you better buy a dog, because you are not going to get it from the employer or the employee. This remarkable prediction is borne out by 1998 U.S. Department of Labor statistics that tell us that 1 of 2 workers today has been working for their current company for less than 1 year and that 2 of 3 workers have been working for the same company for less than 5 years. Add to this that the Secretary of Education, Richard Riley in the Kentucky Teaching and Learning Conferences in Louisville on March 2, 1999, was quoted as saying that none of the top 10 jobs that will be available in the year 2010 exist today, and that these are jobs that will require workers to use technology that has not yet been invented to solve problems that we have not yet thought about.

We are entering an era that increasingly will demand just-in-time learning. This contrasts dramatically with the just-in-case model currently used in most schools—just-in-case it's on the test, just-in-case we might need to use it on the job, just-in-case it might be important. This is because the amount of information coming at us grows almost as quickly as the new technologies. By the time children who are now in kindergarten graduate from 12th grade, a conservative estimate is that information will have doubled itself seven times, and technological power will have doubled itself nearly nine times, producing 256 times more power. Students will still need to learn things, but there will be much less emphasis on the amount of material memorized and much more emphasis on making connections, thinking through issues, and solving problems.

People attending university today will find that half or more of what they learned will be obsolete, outdated, or just plain wrong on the day they graduate. Taking this further, for people attending university early in the 21st century, half of what they learn in any given year will be obsolete by the end of that year. For this reason, learning on a need-to-know basis will become a crucial factor in providing relevant education.

This learning on a need-to-know basis or just-in-time learning parallels what has gone on in business since the early 1980s. There has been a shift in the manufacturing of products to something called "just-in-time delivery." This means that companies no longer stockpile huge warehouses full of inventory but begin to order the materials they need only when a customer orders a product from them.

In the same way, learning will have to shift to just-in-time learning, where information and conceptual material are accessed only when they are needed. We are already seeing this today as businesses try to keep up with the dizzying changes that are taking place in the development of new methods for manufacturing goods, marketing products, and so forth. Many businesses have some workers who are not actually working at any given time. Instead, they are pulled away from their regular duties to learn new techniques, methods, and so on that will soon come into play in their particular jobs. This kind of learning will become much easier when personal, pocket-sized, wireless computer/communicators allow workers to access information from wherever they are when the need arises. This technology will also make it much easier for students to learn in the same way.

Education Will Not Be Confined to a Single Person

Traditionally, a single teacher was the sole source of teaching in the classroom. However, when students have access to technology and information anytime they need it, who they will learn from will radically change. The instantaneous access to people and information will allow students to communicate both locally and globally for instruction. Parents will be able to assist in home-schooling their children whether they are at home or not. Students will be able to contact community and political leaders, business owners, scientists, and a variety of experts from many fields as well as traditional school personnel such as teachers, librarians, counselors, and others from wherever they are.

In addition, language will become less of a barrier to any of these communications. Already, there has been work done on computer software that will take typed text and translate it into any of the major languages in the world. It is not perfect yet, but doubling technological power will result in reliable translation software in the near future. There are personal computers that already respond to verbal commands. Naturally Speaking® and Via Voice® are similar software packages that automatically convert the spoken word into typewritten text as you speak. Although relatively expensive and still early in their development, Moore's Law means that it will only be a short time before voice recognition computers become a common part of our lives. Putting these two concepts together, a software program using voice recognition and automatic language translation will allow individuals to speak in one language to anyone else in the world in the other person's native language. In other words, an English-speaking person could call a Japanese-speaking person and their communication could proceed in both languages while their conversation is automatically interpreted by the software.

By removing the constraints of physical location and time of day, the new technologies will allow people other than teachers to enhance the instruction of students. Although this development may seem threatening to many in the educational establishment, the positive effects on learning must be considered. Students will benefit from the combined wisdom and experience of many people while they learn new skills and concepts. The new technologies will also create a real-world relevance to the learning process. Students will be presented with different and sometimes opposing views as they research their topics. Learning how to draw their own conclusions from a variety of perspectives in such situations will undoubtedly become an essential life skill.

Education Will Not Be Confined to Human Teachers

As students gain access to a wide variety of teachers, it is a certainty that some of them will not be human. This idea will make many of the older-than-30 crowd feel very uneasy, but the Nintendo generation, who have never had a time in their lives where such technologies have not existed, will take to this like ducks to water.

To understand what is about to happen in terms of the emergence of nonhuman teaching assistants, we once again need to apply our knowledge of Moore's Law. We simply cannot make our decisions based on what is in existence today because we know that the continuum of technological development means new and more powerful technologies are imminent. We can only look at what exists today as a basis for projecting where technology will be when the students now in kindergarten graduate from our high schools.

What are the key technologies that will develop into the truly powerful nonhuman teaching assistants of the future? It is difficult to provide any definitive answer to this question given the breadth of development happening today. Certainly, technologies capable of making profound changes to the very nature of education will be produced. However, we must consider two key developments that will influence the direction nonhuman instruction might take: expert systems or smart agents and hypermation.

Consider expert systems or smart agents first. An *expert system* or *smart agent* is a computer program that is given general rules for its operation as well as the capacity to learn from experience. In this way, the program increases its power as it tackles specific problems. One example of this would be a system programmed to diagnose engine problems in cars. Such a system is connected to car dealerships worldwide via satellite. Each day, every problem a dealership encounters is entered into the program as well as the way that problem was solved. When a mechanic encounters a problem, the expert system can give advice by applying the rules in its program as well as by using its growing memory banks. In this way, the expert system has become a valuable reference and learning tool that can be used daily by mechanics anywhere around the world.

Is this what you think a computer is? You will have to look beyond what exists today if you really want to see the role that technology will play in the future of education.

This type of program could have an enormous impact on education. In Chapter 7, we discussed the trend toward miniaturization that will result in powerful, personal, pocket-sized devices capable of instant worldwide communication. If these computer communicators were equipped with smart agents, they would become even more powerful and could be used to find information from any source connected to the worldwide network.

For example, if we were doing research on volcanoes, our personal smart agent could take our verbal request, go out onto the network, and find all incidents of volcanic activity that match our criteria for time, duration, type, and any other attributes we are looking for. This smart agent would learn from experience how we ask questions and what we are really looking for when we phrase our queries in certain ways. In learning our personal habits and tendencies, the smart agent would learn to make connections and inferences from the coexistence of two or more events with similar attributes. Imagine the power this kind of technology would have in the hands of students of all ages.

Once again, we must consider the impact of Moore's Law as it applies to the amount of information available on the global network combined with the increasing sophistication of information technologies. Students will have immediate access from anywhere in the world to information that is more up-to-date than any encyclopedia or textbook anywhere. Personal smart agent technology, combined with the global digital network, will render the traditional role of the teacher as disseminator of information superfluous.

However, these smart agents will do more than just get information. They will also be able to analyze what they find. A student could set an agent to work at monitoring the stock market for any combination of simultaneous ups and downs in various industries, have it watch worldwide arms shipments and terrorist activities, or examine the relationship between the destruction of the rain forest in South America and the depletion of the ozone layer.

The power of this kind of technology to alter education simply cannot be ignored. Much of the traditional education in schools today involves getting information. In fact, so much time and effort is focused on just finding the information that there is little time left over for teaching students how to process, synthesize, and evaluate what is found. In an instructional environment that includes personal smart agents, this problem would be addressed: Teachers would be able to spend more time on the higher-level thinking skills associated with evaluating the information retrieved by the smart agents.

This development should be welcomed by a teaching profession who has for years bemoaned the lack of time and resources needed to teach higher-level thinking skills. As a consequence, in the rapidly emerging new instructional setting, teaching higher-level thought processes will become the focus by default as the technology removes concerns about the amount of informational resources and the speed of access.

Now consider the work being done on the development of hypermation learning systems that we discussed in Chapter 6 combined with personal, pocket-sized computer communicators and smart agents. Students will be able to use a personal learning system that knows how they learn. It will continuously adapt to their needs as they read new material and encounter various difficulties. Such technologies will greatly reduce the lineup at the teacher's desk of students waiting to get some help with the reading or math problems they are working on.

The power of this kind of personal learning system cannot be underestimated. Although not commonly available today, the speed at which these systems will appear will be remarkable. Educators must immediately begin to prepare for a new learning environment where nonhuman teaching assistants will take over many of the tasks currently done by human teachers.

Again, many may see this as a threat, but it need not be so. These teaching assistants will actually free the teacher from the burden of being the source of a great quantity of low-level learning. Such technologies will enable students to learn the alphabet, times table, spelling, and other such tasks with minimal assistance from the teacher. The teacher will then be free to work on the higher-level learning that is currently neglected in the traditional classroom. The future will not see teachers replaced; rather, technology will create the long desired and needed shift in the instructional role that the teacher plays.

Education Will Not Be Confined to Paper-Based Information

As education becomes a system that is no longer limited by time and location and as new technologies become integrated with digital learning technologies, the use of paper will decrease in the classroom. For some, this may seem difficult to accept because although we live in a multimedia generation, the dissemination of information in schools is still essentially paper based. It will not be long, however, until the trends outlined in this book begin to work in concert to produce a new digital reality. As strategic alliances between communications and media companies continue to develop new products and services, digital information and learning technologies will become the norm in schools.

Technologies that bring the world into our homes will soon allow children to wander through the pyramids, visit the rings of Saturn, see chemical reactions at the atomic level, and participate in real-time teleconferencing. None of these experiences will involve paper, but they all will involve learning.

When students go to school, it is difficult to get them interested in the 2-dimensional world of paper. That is because they live in a digital, 3-dimensional, interactive video world outside the classroom. Out there, they are already saturated with light and electrons, so paper and ink are not really in sync with their everyday reality. Educators and schools have to focus on this point of incongruity. Children today get up in the morning to watch television, play interactive games, go to 3-D worlds using Nintendo and PlayStation, go around the world using the World Wide Web, or pick up photos from Mars. They then go to school where they are confronted with all the power of a blackboard or photocopied worksheet. No wonder schools are out of sync with the world that children experience. Unless we pay attention, this situation will only get much worse.

Education Will Not Be Confined to Memorization

Academic success in the Industrial Age was based on a student's ability to memorize facts. People who could suck up and regurgitate information on demand were highly regarded and rewarded. However, this kind of intellectual and informational bulimia does not adequately prepare a person for the Information and Communication Age that we live in. The day when all the information that existed could be stuffed into a person's brain is long gone. As the amount of information continues to double, academic success will depend less and less on rote learning and more and more on a student's ability to process information and use it in a discerning manner.

Memorize, memorize, memorize, and then spill it out on the test before you forget it. If you did well on this exercise you were considered smart.

There will be a shift away from rote learning as the primary means of transmitting knowledge. This means that academic success will increasingly be equated with real learning rather than memorization. In the old system, the emphasis was on getting students ready for tests; in the new emerging system, the emphasis will be primarily on applying what is learned, solving problems, and demonstrating the transfer of learning to new situations. Today, much information has a very short shelf life and therefore quickly becomes disposable. This implies that content specialization must give way to more general knowledge. In other words, as we shift from rote learning to more significant learning, we will witness a parallel shift from specialists to generalists who have the effective analytical processing skills needed to deal with such transient information. This means that our success in the future will not rely just on what we can remember but it will also rely on what we can perceive about the information we are working with and how we can apply this to real-world situations.

⌈ Education Will Not Be Confined to Linear Learning

A society that is based on an assembly line model does not like starting in the middle. The logical sequence was once from beginning to end, and this was the only way to do things. Until the digital age, televisions reflected this philosophy. If there were eight channels and you wanted to get from Channel 3 to Channel 7, you had to first turn the dial through Channels 4, 5, and 6. Channel 4 was only connected to Channels 3 and 5, Channel 5 was only connected to Channels 4 and 6, Channel 6 was only connected to Channels 5 and 7, and so on. Now that we have digital channel changers, we can jump directly from Channel 3 to Channel 7 and back again without ever having to go through the channels in between. As a result, every channel is directly connected to every other channel, just like information systems and the World Wide Web allow virtually any idea to be directly connected to any other idea.

Linear learning is compatible with the assembly line model. Learning is done left to right, top to bottom, beginning to end. This is a lineal, logical, and sequential model. With the introduction of new technologies, however, the learner can start an information expedition in the middle of the material and move backward or forward through the information as needed. As technology creates an interconnected world, people can construct their own learning webs and personal pathways. They can learn what they need when they need it without the interference of unnecessary and irrelevant information. As education and technology visionary David Thornburg said at the Computer Using Educators of California Conference in May 1999, "people will be able to move through conceptual space at the speed of thought."

Education Will Not Be Confined to the Intellectual Elite

Until recently, the real power in our country was in the hands of the *literati*—the people of paper. Increasingly, that power has been transferred to the *clickerati, mouserati,* and *digerati* (for example, people such as Microsoft's Bill Gates, the 90-million-dollar-a-day man). This is because they have developed smart devices that bridge the gap between humans and technology. As a result, technology has become the great equalizer, allowing ordinary people to do extraordinary things. People who understand how to use the Internet can become ad hoc specialists in any field because they have access to high-level information. That information can theoretically give them postgraduate degree-level information in any field. The technology also puts unprecedented power into the hands of ordinary people. For example, a home-based business owner using multimedia publishing technology combined with the most up-to-date information from the World Wide Web could develop proposals and presentations that could rival anything produced by major corporations.

Technology has changed the way we view the intellectual elite and has led to a generational shift in the concept of being "disabled." Technology has allowed people with physical and mental challenges to work and produce in ways that we have never before imagined, empowering them to rise above their disabilities. In the future, it is possible that the definition of *disability* will reflect a person's ability to interact with technology. As a result, people with visible handicaps who embrace technology will no longer be considered disabled. Instead, we will have to deal with the newly disabled: those who are technologically impaired, unable to learn, or unwilling to change as the world changes around them. As a result, our fearless prediction is that in the early part of the 21st century, it is likely that we will view those who are media illiterate, informationally illiterate, or technologically illiterate the same way we view people now who cannot read or write the printed word.

Education Will Not Be Confined to Childhood

In the past, when information had a much longer shelf life, learning was something that was done once in your youth. Then you were done with learning for life. In the good old days, what you learned in your youth prepared you for your single career. Today, learning has become a lifelong process. Given the rapidly changing nature of our world, people of all ages must constantly learn and relearn what they need to know. What they learned yesterday may no longer be valid in tomorrow's world. Tomorrow, they will have to learn again because today's information will already be out of date. Embracing lifelong learning will be a personal and professional imperative for life in the 21st century.

Continual learning is essential for everyone if we are going to have any hope of keeping up with the new technological power.

Education Will Not Be Confined to Controlling Learners

In the Industrial Age, the traditional educational mind-set used a predetermined, predefined, generic cookie-cutter curriculum that led to a one-size-fits-all approach to learning. Unfortunately, this approach did not work for many people. Using this perspective, we thought there must be something wrong with the people who did not fit the system. Today, we understand that we must customize the learning to the individual because different people learn in different ways and at different rates.

Given the traditional approach of controlling learners in a defined environment, educators have had to become fire fighters managing the blaze and maintaining the perimeter. In so doing, some people have suggested that educators have become overzealous and, in some cases, have extinguished students' love of learning completely. Educators must abandon this fire-fighting mentality. Instead, in this new era, our job should be to become arsonists, creating a roaring blaze of passion for learning in all of our students that will sustain itself not just until the next class or term but for a lifetime. Learning can no longer be confined to controlling learners. It needs to become a lifelong empowerment process, and technology can help create the customized learning experiences that have personal relevance for students.

Now that we have an idea of the impact that technology will have on our current school system, let us now turn our attention to the skills, knowledge, understanding, and behaviors that students will need to develop to function effectively in this new environment of the 21st century.

9

Window 9
New Skills for Students

What skills will the graduating classes of the early 21st century need not just to survive but to thrive in this environment of accelerating, technologically driven change? We already understand that because the processing power and speeds of technologies are doubling at incredible rates, access to information will soon be at our fingertips anywhere and at anytime. This suggests that the new curriculum for the new era will have to make a fundamental shift away from a focus on content-driven learning to a far more process-oriented form. As a result, content knowledge will increasingly take a backseat to process skills in student learning. In the future, the skill of learning itself will become the crucial process skill needed for survival.

What skills that we already teach will remain? It should be of no surprise that the three Rs—reading, writing, and arithmetic—will continue to be central to all student learning. This is because they are the essential process skills in a world that is more than ever driven by text and numerical data. Stop for a moment and consider what we really teach when we teach students to read. Do we teach a student to read a single document, or do we teach them the process of reading so that they can go on and read material we never dreamed of when we began? The reading process skills we develop in children will be put to use in the future with reading things we can hardly imagine today. The writing process skills we teach them today will be used to write things well beyond our current comprehension. The math process skills we introduce to our students will allow them to compute well beyond our present capabilities. Process skills empower a person to become independent from their teacher, and process skills last a lifetime. The three skills of reading, writing, and arithmetic are and will remain the basic process skills needed by all our students. However, these in and of themselves will not be enough. We must at least add the following nine process skills to the learning experience of all students.

---

1. Problem Solving and Critical Thinking

This set of process skills must be the foundation of all curriculum. The traditional, Industrial Age education was designed to teach people to follow directions to fit into the stable, assembly line world. Traditional curriculum focuses far less on problem solving and more on simple recall. This approach simply cannot foster the essential problem-solving and process skills needed in a world of constant change. As a result, too many of today's students suffer from "worksheet-itis." To prepare people for the new Information and Communication Age, we must teach them to think for themselves.

Our key responsibility to our graduates is to send them into the world adequately prepared to live and work. To do this, we must understand the needs of the labor market. Employers constantly comment on the inability of young people to think through a problem to the solution on their own. They complain that young workers wait to be told what to do. Just like fish out of water, young people working at their first jobs have moved from the predictable, controlled, and unchanging environment of school to the unpredictable, uncontrolled, rapidly changing environment of the workplace, a world where thinking on one's feet, solving problems independently, and producing results daily are critical. Is it any wonder that they feel lost?

How do we address this concern? First, students should be presented with a real-life problem at their level of development and

Today, there is no more important skill for students to gain than effective problem solving. It is the key to their independence in the modern workplace.

understanding, but most important, students need to be equipped with a systematic, structured process to follow that will enable them to successfully solve problems, regardless of the content area. The process Ted has developed for his students is called the "4Ds." It is based on the structured thought process found in systems analysis and design, and it has proven to be effective in virtually every area of human endeavor. This process involves four distinct steps that lead to effective solutions to problems. The four steps are define, design, do, and debrief.

Define

Students must be taught to define a task so that the problem is fully understood before work begins. How many times have you seen someone waste time working on the wrong task? Thus students must learn to clearly define the task to be done and then confirm their understanding before proceeding any further. This is a valuable life skill. In addition, by turning the responsibility for defining a task over to the students, we force them to use a variety of higher-level thinking skills as they determine what needs to be done.

In the traditional approach to instruction, teachers do the defining and designing of work for their students. Assignments are often presented as something already half finished, with the questions and the directions for finding the solution already in place. This fosters and maintains a culture of student dependency on the teacher to provide the appropriate materials and information. The real world simply does not work this way, and by teaching in this manner, we prevent students from learning to think independently.

Design

Once a problem has been defined, students must then design a solution. Often, this will require students to learn new skills or acquire new information to be able to successfully accomplish the task. The goal in this step is to have the students themselves determine what they need to learn to accomplish the task they have been given. This is a key to fostering independent thinking in students. They will not be able to depend on teachers when they enter the workplace, so we need to begin giving the responsibility for learning to them before they leave us. This means new roles for teachers. If students are given the job of determining what needs to be learned to accomplish the task they have been given, it becomes the job of the teacher to craft the problems so that they lead students to the material in the curriculum that needs to be covered. It also means that teachers must become guides who point students in the right direction after they have determined what they need to learn.

Do

Once a problem has been defined and a plan for its solution has been designed, students must then put the plan into action. This could mean participating in a debate, writing a story, building a desk, writing an essay, baking a cake, doing an experiment, or creating a multimedia presentation. Whatever the task, the students must apply the learning that took place in the design step to do some real work.

Debrief

This is a step that is often overlooked in education. However, determining whether you have actually accomplished what you set out to do is an essential part of learning. It provides useful feedback that helps students do better next time. Continual feedback and performance reviews are just two examples of how the debrief step is built into the procedures of many businesses that are striving for excellence from their employees. Students should get feedback on both the product they have developed and the process they followed in creating it if we want them to get accustomed to the environment of continual improvement they will surely face after graduation.

In every stage of the 4Ds approach, learning involves real-world relevance. Students quickly see the worth in applying their problem-solving skills to real-world tasks. This fosters ownership of the problem-solving process and leads to a culture of autonomy. Repeated and systematic application of the 4Ds empowers independent thinkers. When students are consistently taught to learn through this problem-solving approach, they enter the real world knowing what to do when they encounter the problems they are certain to face.

Although we cannot expect students in kindergarten to have this set of skills, it is reasonable to expect them from all students by the time they reach grade 12. Developing this set of process skills should be a curriculum goal applied through a combination of repeated practice together with a policy of progressive withdrawal. Using this approach, teachers first walk younger students through the process step by step, but as students get more experienced in applying the 4Ds to problem solving, teachers progressively withdraw from supporting students, expecting them to do more and more of the work independently. By the time these students reach grade 12, they should have the necessary skills to allow them to work through real-life problems independent of their teachers.

As we mentioned, graduates of the traditional school system find themselves steeped in a culture of dependency. From kindergarten through grade 12, they have been in a system that has reinforced the idea that content and memorization taught by rote learning is more important than thinking itself. When we take this system away from our students at graduation, we should not be surprised to see that they are unable to stand on their own. As we begin to make the transition from traditional teaching methods to a problem-solving approach for all students, we must learn to gradually let go. It is like watching small children learning to walk. They fall often, but eventually they are able to move around on their own. When it comes to these problem-solving process skills, we must equip students with an understanding of the 4D approach and then let go of them so that they can fall and make mistakes. In this way, we can provide guidance and feedback to help students become better problem solvers while they are still in school.

⌐ 2. Communication Skills

Communication skills are vital for survival in the 21st century. Reading and writing are the two essential communication skills that have long been the cornerstone of the traditional education system. However, in today's emerging Information and Communication Age, being able to speak and listen are just as important, if not more so. As the member of a family, while in the community, or while working in a business, what do we do more of—reading and writing or speaking and listening?

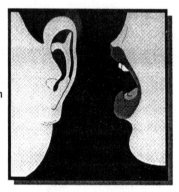

Speaking and listening are important skills to acquire in the preparation of becoming an effective and contributing member of a family, community, and workforce.

Clearly, it is the latter. In a typical day, the average person will speak 18,000 words, which is the equivalent of a 54-page book. Yet in schools, we focus our instruction on reading and writing skills. The skills we use most in everyday life (speaking and listening) are the skills that are taught least. Although these comments should not be interpreted as diminishing the value of reading and writing, it should also be clear that teaching students the necessary skills for effective speaking and listening are as essential as those of reading and writing and that these skills must be explicitly taught at all grades and in all subject areas.

⌐3. Technical Reading and Writing

Technical reading and writing involves a fundamentally different cognitive process that requires a very different set of skills than those used for literary reading and writing. The difference between literary reading and technical reading is the difference between reading a novel or poem and reading a computer screen or technical manual. The difference between literary writing and technical writing is the difference between writing an essay about plot development in *Hamlet* and writing a set of technical instructions for programming a VCR to record a program while the owner is out of the house. Technical reading and writing was once considered to be solely the domain of technicians and related wireheads; a job they did not do that well, by the way. However, given the amount of technology in our world, technical reading and writing has now become a process skill that everyone must be expected to master. With the constant doubling in the power of technology combined with the exponential growth of information we can expect to experience in our lifetimes, we must be able to deal with new technical issues and ideas as they appear. Frequently, we must be able to work with new technologies, often teaching ourselves and our coworkers the things we need to know.

Literary reading and writing skills are and will continue to be important to the learning process. However, equal weight must be given to technical reading and writing skills as they apply to the curriculum. It is not a question of allowing students to choose whether they prefer reading novels or software manuals because this is not an either/or situation. Both sets of skills will be absolutely necessary. Technical reading and writing must not be taught in isolation if educators are to ensure that all students are equipped for success in the modern technical world. These are skills that must be taught at the highest level of integration in all subject areas and at all grade levels.

⌐ 4. Applied Technical Reasoning Skills

Again, stop for a moment and ask yourself the following questions: What do you think will happen over the course of the next few years? Will there be less technology or more technology in our lives? Although many people wish the answer was *less*, it is a certainty that there will be lots more. If this is so, then applied technical reasoning skills will undoubtedly be essential skills to teach students to prepare them for our increasingly technological world.

So just what do we mean by technical reasoning skills? People with technical reasoning skills understand more than just how something works; they can apply their understanding to real-world situations. For example, they can apply theoretical science and mathematics to real-world problems to come up with the solutions to them. It is not necessarily about everyone becoming a scientist but about everyone being scientifically literate. In the same way, they can apply statistics, logic, and probability to a variety of real-life, real-time situations and feel comfortable using statistical numerical systems. Here again, it is less about becoming a mathematician than it is about becoming mathematically literate in the most common application of mathematics in everyday life. In addition, they are confident that they can learn whatever technical knowledge they do not have because they possess the process skills that allow them to quickly learn what is necessary. More than anything else, they can apply what they know to real work.

Although in much of the rest of the industrialized world, the term *applied* refers to applying theory to real-life situations, in North America, *applied* has long been a euphemism for *easier*. In the minds of many educators, the term *applied* refers to a set of lower-level skills taught to less able students. The problem with this perspective is that it is extremely difficult to apply something you do not understand. In reality, application is a higher-level thinking skill than just learning theory. For example, in Bloom's Taxonomy of Higher Order Thinking Skills, application is considered to be a higher skill than simply knowing facts. It is hard to actually apply something we do not know or understand.

One way to help students develop applied reasoning skills is to engage them in hands-on learning experiences involving technology. Although it would be wonderful for our students to have access to state-of-the-art, high-end technology, we can provide them with the same or similar experiences with solutions that are far more low tech in nature. Technology is far more than computers. Furthermore, a great many technology concepts can be taught using fairly basic equipment such as phones and blenders. However, we must not stop there. If we want our students to be prepared for the real world of today, we must have a progression in our curriculum that moves from focusing on individual tools to examining systems. The Industrial Age mind-set broke life down into individual items and then focused on them. What we now want our students to grasp is the interconnected, interdependent nature of how things function in real settings. There are a great many resources in the community that can help us do this. For example, ask your local telephone company to donate old telephones and have your students put them together to learn about electricity and electronics, ask a local technician to show students how to disassemble a VCR or clock radio, or take your students on a tour of the local electrical plant, water purification system, or telephone switching station.

As things stand, the whole realm of logic, probability, and statistics gets very little attention in the traditional curriculum. This clearly has to change and change quickly because these skills are going to play an increasingly important role in our lives. And like critical thinking, problem solving, communication, and technical reading and writing skills, these skills need to be taught at the applied rather than just the theoretical level. Why? Anyone who took algebra or trigonometry in high school or college understands that if you do not apply it, you lose the ability to do it. How many of you could pass the algebra or trig test you took way back when? Exactly!

---

5. Information Literacy

Consider what comes into our homes these days. In the March 9th, 1998, issue of *Business Week,* it was reported that almost 98% of homes in America today have a color television, 97% have a radio, and 96% have a telephone. In addition, increasingly homes have access to cable and the World Wide Web. Add to these all of the print-based information in newspapers, magazines, journals, and so forth and it can easily be seen that we are bombarded with information. However, much, if not most, of the material that inundates us has no significance attached to it. We actually live in the age of a raw-data explosion rather than an age of the explosion of information. For it to truly inform us, we need to be able to see the importance of the data we receive.

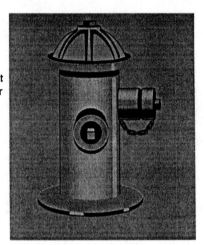

The sheer volume of water coming out of a fire hydrant makes it unusable for getting a drink: The amount of water would overwhelm you! In the same way, the wide variety of information sources in the new Information and Communication Age we now live in overwhelm us with the volume of news they send us.

In times such as these, the ability to manage and work with information is quickly becoming a survival skill. Those who are not able to manage the flow inevitably end up suffering from information overwhelm and exhaustion. As Richard Wurman indicates in his book, *Information Anxiety* (1990), like someone forced to drink water from a gushing fire hydrant, the sheer volume of information coming at us completely engulfs us. When this happens, information becomes ineffective and even useless. When we are unable to make sense of the data we are drowning in, it is extremely difficult to get beyond the data to knowledge. In the Information Age, we need the ability to find and apply significant information. The toughest part is being able to differentiate the important from the unimportant bits of data. People do not just need to know what the data says; they need to understand its impact and significance so it can become information.

How do we do this? The answer lies in acquiring a complete set of information literacy skills with which to access, analyze, authenticate, and apply the information so that we can turn it into useful, personal knowledge. We must equip students growing up in this world of data explosion with these skills. The first step is to teach them how to systematically integrate strategic and logical question asking and searching techniques into their daily information retrieval activities. Students must learn that it is the quality of the questions they ask that determine the quality of their research. In doing this, students begin to understand the importance of moving beyond just getting the right answers to being able to ask the right questions.

Obviously, in the modern world, students must also learn to transparently access information from a variety of sources worldwide. They should be able to do research not only on the World Wide Web but also through a wide selection of electronic and nonelectronic resources. However, information literacy goes well beyond asking where to get the information. It must also include asking how to organize and present the knowledge that is acquired. Students must consider the appropriate medium or media needed to present the material retrieved and processed for specific projects. The idea here is to make certain that they understand the wide variety of means through which they can communicate their learning. These might include audio and video clips, a verbal presentation or debate, or a written essay that might include graphics to illustrate important points.

Educators must recognize that we live in an intensely graphical world that makes the use of images, sounds, and video clips a basic part of the communication process. Educators have long known that the final step in the writing process is the presentation of material to the intended audience. Teachers in the elementary grades understand this and encourage their students to enhance the communication of their writing with pictures, color, and decoration. Unfortunately, much of this is lost as students progress into high school where the emphasis shifts almost exclusively to the writing itself. The real world of modern information dissemination is a colorful multimedia experience where graphic design is used to enhance the communication of content. It is so much a part of how information is communicated today that people simply expect effective graphic design to be an integral part of what they read or view. The print and electronic media industries have recognized this expectation and have responded appropriately. It is time for educators to catch up, both in the learning materials we produce and in the way we teach all students to communicate their ideas. An understanding of the principles of graphic design should be taught to all students as an integral part of the communication process.

Understanding the power of graphic design in publishing, video, and multimedia communications must be a fundamental component of a student's basic literacy education in the modern world, both for communicating ideas and for intelligently processing the messages being targeted at them. As students develop an understanding of the visual world and the principles of visual literacy, they can begin to recognize how information can be shaped to manipulate us. Tragically, far too many people do not really understand how the increasingly graphical world they live in is being used to bias the messages they receive.

We must acknowledge that the Information Age requires a new set of cognitive skills for information processing. Most adults are text and paper trained. In addition, we grew up in a world that was lineal, logical, and sequential (left to right, top to bottom, beginning to end). The new generation is light and sound trained. This is a world of hypertext, images, and sound where information can be processed like you are in the center of a web: You can move forward, backward, or sideways at will. Although we learned to think and write with ink and lead, students today need to learn to think and write with electrons. This involves a fundamentally different cognitive process that compels us to redefine the true meaning of information literacy from the traditional text and still picture curriculum of our past to the multimedia world of the Information Age that has already engulfed us.

---

6. Technology as a Tool

There is a widespread misconception that technology is a subject or curriculum. This is absolutely wrong. The issue is not about teaching Microsoft Word™, AppleWorks™, or Hyperstudio™. It is not even about the cards, cables, RAM or ROM, or input or output issues that fascinate many. What it is really about is using technology as a tool to help us be more productive. In fact, the term *technology* is misleading. It seems that we apply the term only to those things that were invented after we were born. For example, we do not call a refrigerator technology and spend hours pondering what refrigeration is doing to the nature of food, and we do not consider a piano as technology and wonder what it is doing to the essence of music. The problem is that many of our generation can remember a time when much of the stuff that we are dealing with today did not exist. For our children—for the Nintendo generation—there has never been a time in their lives when VCRs, CD players, satellites, cell phones, computers, and the Internet have not existed. They have always been there. If we have having trouble dealing with this, it is our problem, and it is time for us to get over it and get on with things. We do not ponder the pencil and wonder about how they got the lead in there. It is transparent, and unless it is broken or we cannot find it, we do not dwell on the pencil but we focus on the task. This applies equally as well to the use of electronic technology in the learning process.

Technology is not important in and of itself. It is what the technology can do to make you more productive in your daily tasks that is important.

For education, the central issue is about how technology can be organized around student learning, not how student learning can be organized around technology. We need to see technology as helping students think and communicate effectively. If a device can do something better, more efficiently, more accurately, or quicker than we can do it manually, why not use it? Isn't that the true purpose of technology? It is only when we learn to get beyond the tool and begin to focus on the task that we will really be able to appreciate and understand the power of the device. People today use cars, electricity, and a multitude of other technologies to make their lives more pleasant and efficient. We are not conscious of these things; we simply let the technology empower us to do much more than we could do without it. Most of the time the technology we use is transparent.

If new electronic technology will empower us to do much more than ever before, we must make a major shift in how we approach its use. We must learn to let go of the mechanical things technology can do for us and concentrate on the things that the technology cannot do. Many teachers find this sort of statement unnerving. This is because there is a great deal of concern expressed that students should not become too dependent on technology to do their spelling and basic arithmetic calculations. It is here, where technology begins to enter the cognitive realm, that it makes some of us uncomfortable. Although a student of the past may have been able to add, subtract, divide, and multiply better than a student will in the future, the student of the future will be able to do these operations faster and more accurately using electronic technology. This is because tomorrow's students will not struggle with technology; rather, they will allow it to empower them. Consider how students play video games. They are not concerned with how the joystick works, they use it intuitively, and they focus instead on what the joystick does. In the same way, the focus with technology needs to shift from the tools to how the capabilities of these new tools will empower students to do new things. This will free them to go places that we never had the opportunity to go ourselves. In the years ahead, technology will not be the focus but simply the vehicle that takes the student of the future farther than the student of the past could ever imagine.

To begin this process, we must stop teaching things such as keyboarding and word processing as separate subjects. These should be considered simply a part of the communications process and taught incidentally in the teaching of the writing process in language arts, science, and social studies classes. As the use of technology becomes an ordinary part of our lives and the lives of our children, educators will find that the technology will become increasingly transparent, just like the pencil. All that will be left is for the student to focus on the task while the technology works in the background.

At the same time, educators must get over the idea that technology will replace them. Any teacher that can be replaced by a computer absolutely deserves to be because they just do not get it. Simply stated, we could put a state-of-the-art device on the desk of every student, teacher, administrator, and superintendent in every district in this nation, but if that is all we did, the only thing that would change is the power bill would get a lot bigger. Without the vision and understanding of an inspired educator, little else of value would happen. Education is a human task that cannot be delegated solely to computers. Although these new electronic tools have great power, we must not confuse the tool with the task because technology in and of itself does not and cannot improve the human condition; only humans can improve the human condition. The critical question must be where and how we can best use technology to help us on the road to knowledge.

⌐ 7. New Personal Skills

Global competition, the doubling of technological power, and the explosion of information in the modern world has created an absolute economic pressure cooker for business and industry. No longer do we have the stability that was common even as little as 20 years ago. In a global economy where everything is directly connected to everything else, every time the yen, Eurodollar, mark, or dollar changes value, business plans have to be completely reworked. This has led to a rapid and dramatic change in the nature of the workplace. Companies based on being big and predictable are rapidly being replaced by organizations that are fast, flexible, quick-change artists. This is reflected in today's workplace. John Walsh, in a February 13, 1998, speech to Vocational Education Teachers in Vancouver, BC, reported from the University of Guelph that for every job created by a company of more than 100 employees, there are 17 jobs being created by companies with less than 8 employees. In such an environment, many of today's students will spend their lives working as digital entrepreneurs. However, we have seen only a hint of the enormous changes that are to come.

One of the major reasons for the dramatic increase in the number of small companies in the economy is the amazing power that is now available to these businesses. Due to the tremendous gains in efficiency from electronic technology, Frank Koelsch (1995), in his book *Infomedia Revolution,* has projected that in the next 5 years, we will see changes in productivity on the order of ½ by 2 by 3. This means that half as many people will be paid twice as much money to produce three times as much value. Continual development of new and more powerful electronic tools has made the business world an exciting, rapidly changing, and unstable environment.

There are new and basic skills that students must master if they are going to succeed in the world of tomorrow. These skills include many personal skills such as time management, self-assessment, and entrepreneurship.

For workers, dealing with this ever-changing playing field where the balance of power is shifting quickly in favor of small business means that coping with ambiguity and fundamental uncertainty will become the norm. To survive, companies of the future will increasingly contract out large portions of their business. Trends such as this tell us that as many as 80% of today's kindergarten students will have to be their own employers. To survive, let alone thrive in such an environment, they will need to be equipped with a very different set of skills than that of the previous generation.

First and foremost, this means that teaching students how to be independent will be a critical outcome that must guide educators as they prepare students for the rest of their lives. This will require a major shift in mind-set as we embrace a whole new skill set that people will need for success in this new business environment. People who work as entrepreneurs must learn how to be self-motivators, self-learners, and self-assessors. They will need to learn about such things as goal setting, time management, stress management, teamwork, self-marketing, presentation making, financial management, negotiation skills, and 21st century communications skills. We will have to make a huge shift in emphasis in how and what we teach our students to make our instruction relevant in the modern, competitive world of powerful small business.

8. New Mind-Set Skills

As a result of these changes, everyone will need to learn to live life like a quarterback and anticipate the future. Thus, we will need to develop strategies for passing this important mind-set skill on to our students. Developing their intuition about where things are going will be critical because learning will not be just about learning new skills; it will also be about learning to let go of old skills that no longer work the way they once did. Getting rid of old, ineffective skills will help remove some of the barriers that might prevent us from seeing things from different perspectives. To do this requires students to practice the principles of organized abandonment and to learn how to undo their previous thinking, creating space for new ideas. If they cannot do this, they will have difficulty learning the new things they must learn in the short time they will have to learn them.

In the new millennium, experience will not be as valuable as it used to be. The ability to adjust, adapt, and leverage what you know will matter as much as the experience you have gained. In fact, there are already managers today that look at long résumés with a critical eye because too much experience in one company or with one way of doing business may indicate that an individual has become married to a paradigm, and this may mean a person is not as open to change as they need to be. This is a complete inversion of the Industrial Age thinking that still pervades our society. Instead of staying the course and valuing the way we have always done something, now we need to be always on the hunt for new ideas that could reinvent our business or organization. As declared in the title of Robert Kreigel's book *If It Ain't Broke, Break It,* in the fast paced competitive modern world, if we do not, somebody else will.

Now just stop for a moment and think about what this means for equipping students with the right skills needed for continual success. Again, a major shift in how we approach this thing called edu-

Students need the ability to live life as a quarterback—to perceive the future before it happens. This is a fundamental skill for success in the modern world that we must pass on to our students.

cation will be required. Students will need the mind-set skills necessary for dealing with rapid change. We will need to teach our students how to continually be thinking "outside the box." As renowned business consultant Tom Peters says in his speeches, this will mean teaching students how to understand and appreciate the value of crazy, stupid, completely off-the-wall ideas. If an idea seems crazy or stupid, it is often because it is outside our personal or company paradigm. We must learn to overcome our desire to immediately dismiss these ideas and give them careful consideration. Staying competitive often means coming up with crazy, nonlinear ideas.

We must help students develop their thinking and intuition skills and encourage them to change their mind-sets often. Using a different mind-set unlocks a whole new way of thinking and seeing things. The contributions made to our world by the likes of Stephen Hawking and Albert Einstein began with a change of mind-set. It was their new approach to a problem that was the key to their success.

Understanding this, we need to appreciate the value of useful failure as a teaching tool. The essence of innovation is the pursuit of failure. Consequently, failing can be a good exercise, as long as it is productive. In business today, the message is that if you do not fail, then you are not succeeding. Learning from a mistake means we can move on and try something else that will work better. To understand this, we should take a lesson from the past. On December 31, 1879, Thomas Edison demonstrated his most famous invention: the first practical incandescent electric lamp. To get to that point, he had experienced hundreds of failures. When it was suggested by his assistant that he must feel like a failure, Edison replied by simply saying that he now knew hundreds of ways how *not* to make a light bulb. In the end, he was successful because he persisted and learned from his failures. We must now teach students today that failing can be a good thing.

---

9. A Beef Stew Curriculum

In the earliest part of this century, Henry Ford used Eli Whitney's principles of mass production to create the automobile assembly line. As we have already discussed, this resulted in workers being assigned to a task that they were expected to complete as quickly and accurately as they could, in a machine-like manner. Working in such a system, each worker was only responsible for his or her specific task. Workers were not expected to think or concern themselves with the bigger picture of what happened to the product before they received it or after it left their hands. Concern about the finished product was left to the 15% of the workforce who made up the management of the company. These were the select few who were paid to use their minds rather than just their hands. The increased levels of productivity that resulted from the application of these principles were so astonishing that within a very short time, they were applied widely across institutions throughout North America, including the public school system.

In the past, we broke learning into separate subjects and taught them one at a time, much like eating different foods on a dinner plate. But life is an interrelated stew of experiences in which we get more than a single thing in a bite.

As a direct result of this decision, in very short order, learning became compartmentalized and life began to be taught as a series of separate subjects. For a long time, this model worked as well in schools as it did on the production line. However, now at the beginning of the new millennium, we live in a fundamentally different world of work that long ago outgrew the principles of mass production. Yet despite the fact that the world out there has radically changed, most schools continue to teach a meat-and-potatoes curriculum where subjects are taught as separate courses using an assembly line approach to move students along from one specialist to another when the bell rings. How many times have you heard a teacher say, "I don't teach math," or "I only teach senior chemistry," or "It's not my job to teach grammar"? These statements reflect the fact that the school system is still based on the Industrial Age premise of departmentalization. The school system is suffering from a hardening of the categories! Although this worked very well many years ago, this approach is becoming increasingly irrelevant in the world of tomorrow.

What we now understand is that life cannot be fully understood if we just learn about meat and potatoes separately. Rather, life is a stew of interrelated experiences and can be much more fully understood with a holistic approach that makes the connections between what we have previously considered as separate disciplines. Students can sit in math class and have a math experience, but life is about far more than that. It is about how the math of statistics, logic, probability, algebra, and trigonometry connects with music, science, art, social studies, English, and psychology. In the classrooms of tomorrow, the math department will become a sphere of influence that exerts its impact in varying degrees on the various tasks and problems that students tackle in school. As a result, schools will have to move beyond just getting students ready for the next class, next unit, next term, or next year of a subject. We will have to embrace a much more holistic approach.

Educators must understand the power of technology and information to transform everything they teach. They must be willing to accept the problems associated with paradigm paralysis and be willing to do something about it, and they must begin by accepting the challenge of working on acquiring this new set of skills for themselves as well as for their students. Learning these new skills will enable educators to prepare young people for the changing world we must face.

The bottom line is that we must discard the notion that schools can teach everything that all students will need to know in their lives. What we must understand is that learning has now become a life-long process of keeping abreast of change and of learning to learn. This a world where it is not just about earning a living but about learning and relearning a living; it is about learning today, learning tomorrow, and learning forever for our students as well as for ourselves!

10

Window 10
New Roles for Educators

To teach in the system of the future, educators will need more than just a few professional days devoted to technology use; they will need to make a significant shift in their paradigms for teaching and learning. This means new roles for teachers. We must recognize that the traditional system has been set up to prepare students for a world that no longer exists. We must embrace the fact that massive, ongoing retraining for educators is absolutely essential if schools are to be made relevant to the needs of our students.

However, to bring about this substantial change in how teachers view their role in the classroom, we must address two major impediments to teacher retraining. The first is the fact that traditional school culture is not accustomed to change. In fact, the school system is probably one of the most stable institutions existing in the world today: Our school year was set in the 1800s, we have had no real competition for our students, our basic organizational structure was set in the Industrial Age of the assembly line, and the majority of our teachers employ instructional methods that have been used for hundreds of years. Although the rest of the world has undergone radical and repeated restructuring during the past 15 to 20 years, schools have remained amazingly untouched by these sweeping changes.

This has led to a strong resistance to change. Many teachers believe that change happens to someone else.

The second impediment to teacher retraining is the very nature of the job of teaching itself. Despite the perception of much of the public and the media, teaching is a difficult job that is full of stress. Teachers are asked to do a lot, and their plate is already full. Making the kinds of changes we are suggesting here will never happen in the current model of teachers taking 4 or 5 days a year to tackle all of the organizational, instructional, and student behavior problems associated with running a school.

Therefore, schools of the future must embrace the kind of retraining models that have proven effective in the business world. Many company managers have realized that to be effective in reeducating their workforce, they have to remove their workers from their regular work so that they can focus on the task of learning. Many companies have built training centers and have a significant portion of their workers attending retraining classes on an ongoing basis. Schools will have to do the same. Retraining will require ongoing classes for teachers where they are released from their regular teaching duties. If we want to see the kinds of changes necessary to bring schools in line with the new reality, then we have no option but to radically reprioritize and restructure professional development for teachers.

So where do we begin? What are the new skills that all educators must learn to apply to their current professional practices in the new retraining classes they are attending? The essence of the task that lies ahead is the same as it always has been for educators: to help their students learn the relevant skills, knowledge, attitudes, attributes, and behaviors they will need to be good and productive citizens of the nation. To do this effectively, educators will need to apply six new skills.

1. Educators as Futurists

As we have already mentioned, teachers will need to learn to live their lives like quarterbacks, anticipating the future and doing their own trend analysis. Thus they will begin to visualize some of the multitude of possibilities in the world of the future. Again, we are not referring to gazing into a crystal ball. Rather, what we are suggesting is a reasoned extrapolation based on current trends as they unfold. Being able to do this is crucial to keeping the curriculum of the future relevant. As teachers begin to practice this, they are doing more than just staying on top of change. They are also providing students with a good model for how to deal with change.

⌐ 2. Educators as Process Instructors

Educators have long aspired to the teaching of higher-order thinking skills—skills such as analysis, synthesis, and evaluation that are critical to effective problem solving. Unfortunately, dealing with the teaching and assessing of lower-level skills such as memorization of content, basic spelling, grammar, and basic arithmetic takes up so much time, we often do not get to those higher-level skills that we think are so important. It can be very frustrating. However, technology may offer teachers some real hope. New technologies are increasingly being given the capacity to assist in the teaching of lower-level thinking tasks of the curriculum. Using these new tools, educators will be able to explore instruction where more emphasis is placed on the teaching of higher-level process skills.

What is more powerful: Teaching students how to add a set of specific numbers or teaching them the process of addition? The process skill empowers students to go on to perform calculations the teacher never dreamed of when the students were first taught.

There is, however, a major issue that teachers must face if this hope of teaching higher-order thinking skills is to be realized: Educators must be prepared to let go of some lower-level teaching and let it be done by the technology. We have already discussed the need for teachers to embrace a partnership with nonhuman electronic assistants, but this represents a quantum leap for many educators.

There will be great feelings of discomfort and fear of losing control because traditionally teachers have been in charge of all instruction that takes place in the classroom.

These feelings of disorientation are predictable. The rest of the world has been dealing with the phenomenon of technologically induced change for some time. It is important for teachers to realize that instability is a normal consequence of the development of technological power. No matter where it has been applied, the powerful new electronic technology has fundamentally destabilized the status quo. New tools and techniques quickly render traditional methods obsolete. Because the school system has been stable for such a long time, the instability that will result from the use of new electronic tools for instruction will be considerable. Teachers, especially those who have been teaching for a long time, will find the next few years very challenging. However, we must persist because one of the great benefits of the appropriate use of new technological tools is more time for teachers to focus on teaching higher-level skills.

Teaching higher-order thinking skills deals as much with teaching the process of learning as it does with teaching how to create the product of learning. This will require a significant shift in the ways we teach and assess students. It will mean a fundamental shift away from preparing students for pencil-and-paper tests. The content-based approach promotes a teach, test, and turf model where we fill students up with content so that they can regurgitate it on request; then they forget it. This must end. Rather, we need teachers who can teach process together with content and who understand the increasingly disposable nature of information. In the future, the focus will have to be less on the content and the testing of that content and more on the context and the assessing of the ability of students to apply content to real-world experiences.

⌐ 3. Educators as Guides

As we have just discussed, the view that students are vessels to be filled with information is fast becoming an obsolete notion that is a deeply entrenched reflection of a bygone time. In the traditional mind-set, a teacher was a person who knew all there was to know and passed on this knowledge to students. Although this approach worked in the past, this situation no longer applies. Paper-based tests predominantly reflect memory and content, not process thinking and the ability to change paradigms. The competencies needed to function effectively in the face of constant change are incredibly more complex than anything students can learn from a prescribed textbook or demonstrate on a paper-and-pencil test. Technology is changing too rapidly and the amount of information in the world is increasing too quickly for any one person to have complete knowledge in any specific area. It is time to drop the notion of teachers as vessel fillers, and start to consider students as fires to be kindled. As we have mentioned, teachers must become arsonists, igniting a roaring blaze of passion for learning in their students and themselves that sustains itself not just to the next day or class but for a lifetime.

How do we do this? We need to move away from being just the sage on the stage and toward becoming the guide on the side in the classroom. Because we can no longer be the repository for all knowledge, we can become the guides who can point the way. We can teach students how to access information, what to do with information when they get it, and how to use it to solve real-world problems. Once we have walked students through this process, we can begin to slowly and progressively withdraw, and in doing so we can allow students to solve problems for themselves. This means that we must learn to let go, to be less in control in the classroom. Again, as we have just discussed, this is perhaps the most difficult challenge for many teachers because classroom control is the essence of the Industrial Age paradigm of what it means to be a good teacher, and it is often a source of personal pride. Great classroom management skills were necessary in the traditional system where all decisions were made at the top. In such systems, information regurgitation ruled. However, these rules no longer apply.

We need to understand that educators have a new and different role to play as guides, showing students how to follow the trails to learning for themselves or blazing their own trails. Educators must encourage students to go further and in different directions from the traditional beaten paths that learners have always followed. To do this, we need to move away from being classroom controllers and managers and move toward being peer and team learning facilitators. Never has that old saw about giving someone a fish versus teaching them to fish been more appropriate than it is today.

4. Educators as Knowledge Experts

Wisdom is needed to convert information into knowledge. Wisdom has long been considered a higher-order thinking skill that was predominantly the domain of the elderly in our society. These are people who have the perspective of the long view and can apply their wealth of life experience to everyday situations and problems. Today, being a "knowledge expert" has taken on additional meaning. It involves having the ability to stand back and perceive the significance of data and trends. It means being able to apply this understanding to produce real-life knowledge products such as the interpretation of theories, translation of complicated ideas into simpler terms, analysis of the implications of the application of a product or procedure, description of circumstances that theory does or does not explain, creation of demonstrations and simulations to enhance learning, constructive criticism of ideas, methods, and products, and so on. We generally do not lead students to value such skills in our current curriculum.

Wisdom is being able to see beyond the immediate and perceiving the real meanings of events and information. There has never been a time when passing this on to students has been more important.

In the Agricultural Age, society was organized around producing crops. In the Industrial Age, society was organized around producing goods. In the Information Age, technology is moving us toward the production and application of the knowledge-based products we just described. Knowledge experts know how to combine their personal experiences and understanding with new technologies and the most up-to-date information to create knowledge products. They also know how to teach their students to do the same. Increasingly, these are the skills that will be valued in an ever-changing world and thus necessary for us to teach in schools.

5. Educators as Models

Students not only do what we say but they also model what we do. They unconsciously model our thought processes and pick up on what we value. This is an important point often missed by educators. Teachers often demonstrate that they value the product students hand in rather than the thought process required to create it. This can be seen both in how we teach and how we evaluate student learning. Here is a clear example of how this value was conveyed by a math teacher (one of the authors). The situation was the teaching of a proof in a mathematics class. When the teacher reached the end of the proof, it did not work out. He remembers feeling upset, embarrassed, and defeated. As a result, he went away and worked on that proof at home until he could do it forward and backward. In the next math class, when he completed the proof on the board, his students saw only the end result of the learning process he had gone through. They never got to see the struggle, thinking, and mess involved in his solving the problem at home, and his students then felt upset and defeated. It was not until years later that he realized he had done his students a great disservice. He had presented them with a finished product that was unattainable to them because he did not model the learning process they needed to go through to get there.

Students follow what teachers do. If we want them to be continual learners, we need to be learning continually.

In terms of evaluation, many teachers tell their students that product is far more important than process. Here is one example of how they do it. We know that there are five distinct steps in the writing process: planning, drafting, revising, proofing, and publishing. Most teachers know that the key to good writing is to have their students progress through each of the steps in the process. However, when it comes to assessing student learning, they focus completely on the end product, giving little, if any, marks for successfully following through the five steps in the process. The students quickly learn that regardless of what the teacher says, the thing that counts is the final product. No wonder we have trouble getting students to revise their writing once it is done.

When educators place too much emphasis on the product to be created, it really does not help students learn. The bottom line is that learning and thinking is a messy business. The thinking skills in the processes behind the products are what empower the students to do the creating. So those thinking skills need to be our focus. The math teacher mentioned above has since changed his approach, and he now puts much more emphasis on the thinking involved in problem solving. He models everything from asking questions to analyzing possible solutions to working them through even if they do not work out. He has realized that getting students to apply a structured thought process is the key to successfully teaching his students to think mathematically.

Almost as important as what we do is what we do not do. Amazingly, our students also model what we do not do. If you stop and think about it for a moment, you will see that there are three sets of curricula in every classroom. The first is the explicit curriculum as outlined by the state or province. The second is the implicit curriculum that we learn from the teacher's values. The third is what we will call the *null curriculum*—what we learn from what teachers do not do.

Consider the null curriculum as it might apply to the many students today who are told that technology is important, but at the same time work with teachers who do not or will not use it. Even today, in a world profoundly affected by the explosion of technology into our lives, many educators take the attitude that technology might be a great tool, but it is not their job to learn it, use it, or teach it. They see no connection between the subject matter they teach and new technologies. By refusing to see or even consider the connections, trends, and tremendous change engulfing the world, teachers are sending students the unspoken message that technology really is not very important.

Thus, educators must recognize the impact of what we model to our students. We need to focus on the positive power our actions can have in fostering the attitudes and behaviors students need for success.

⌐ 6. Educators as Learners

As the prospect of being an all-knowing teacher fades into the past, educators are beginning to understand that they must make the transition from teaching their students to learning *with* their students and even to learning *from* their students. Transforming our professional practices is a powerful teaching strategy that enables educators to maintain relevance by becoming excellent role models, knowledge experts, learning guides, process instructors, and futurists. Being open to and embracing all the skills necessary for taking on new instructional roles is critical as we move into the new millennium.

If the education system is to survive and rise to the challenges facing it in the 21st century, the system must take on the qualities of a learning organization, and the teachers must take on the qualities of new millennium learners. A learning organization, as defined by Peter Senge in his milestone book, *The Fifth Discipline* (1990), is a community of autonomous people who skillfully, consciously, and responsibly cooperate with others to build the enormous human potential in their dynamic roles as producers, consumers, and community members. A learning organization seeks to create its own future. It assumes learning is an ongoing and creative process. It develops, adapts, and transforms itself in response to the needs and aspirations of the people it connects with.

As educators in the new millennium, we must see ourselves as members of a learning organization where our own learning makes the organization stronger and keeps it relevant. One cannot be static in such an organization. For many teachers, this will mean realizing that there is a big difference between teaching for 15 years and teaching 1 year 15 times. We must recognize that we are in a learning business. As such, we must realize that we will be teaching, but we will also be simultaneously learning with and from our students.

11

Window 11
The Need for Vision

In this book, we have looked through several different windows on the future. We have asked you to consider your own paradigms and the effects these mind-sets have had on how you view and use technology. Understanding the origin and basis of our current paradigms helps open the windows to the future more fully and allows us to make sense of the changes that are at work in the world today. It is only in getting beyond our own paradigm paralysis and embracing new ways of thinking that we can begin to harness the astonishing power of the forces that have been unleashed on us through the proliferation of new technologies. Until and unless we can step back from all that is happening and learn to deal with change and the changing nature of change, simply peering through the windows into the future will leave us as little more than passive observers as the world passes us by. Throughout this book, we have stressed that when looking through windows on the future, it is essential to move beyond seeing to perceiving. This requires the ability to anticipate where things are going and to expect the unexpected. Perceiving the future through what is happening in the present requires vision.

Helen Keller, the great American writer and thinker, was blind, deaf, and mute from early in her life, but she overcame these profound handicaps to become one of America's most eloquent spokespersons for the possibilities of life. Despite her many handicaps, she became a university professor, the author of more than 30 books, and a great visionary. When once asked how she felt about being blind, she responded by stating that there was one thing worse than not being able to see and that was being able to see and having no vision. Her statement applies just as well today when we consider how to deal with the many possibilities of technological change: It requires people with vision.

"There is one thing worse than not
being able to see—it's being able
to see and having no vision."
                        —Helen Keller

Windows on the Future is intended to provide interpretation, understanding, context, and vision to the multitude of changes that are happening as well as to the implications these changes have for our future. Only by asking you to stand back and take the longer view can we begin to understand some of the possibilities that technology holds for our children, schools, communities, businesses, and society at large.

To do this, we stood at one window and looked back into the recent past at the major foundations of the Industrial Age. Through another window, we examined 10 major developments of significance in the human quest for computing power, starting with counting stones right through to today's supercomputers. As we examined these developments, considered the power of Moore's Law and the astounding growth in the processing power of computational devices, and projected what the impact this doubling might have on our future, we were led to another window where we focused on the four major technological trends unfolding in our world today: global digital networks, technological fusion, new strategic alliances, and personal computers for everyone. We then superimposed these multiple views on education past, present, and future to shape a vision of what schools for the new millennium might look like.

What is our message? Education is the major issue in the post-industrial society in which we live. This is fundamentally an issue of national security because schools are our farms of the future. Imagine what would have happened in the Industrial Age if we had run out of iron ore. Imagine what will happen in the new Information Age if we run out of thinking minds, which is a primary resource. Schools produce our most valuable crop—the most essential raw material for our Information Age economy.

So how do we leverage these powerful new technologies to bring about the meaningful and lasting changes in schools that will ensure our continued economic success in the modern changing world? How can we change the curriculum to reflect the growing power of the new devices and mind-sets that they create? How do we retool what is already in place?

We must begin by facing the facts. We live in a new and very different world, one that is constantly recreating and redefining itself. Changing our schools is absolutely essential if our children are to be properly prepared for the world that awaits them. For this reason, education cannot be approached as a "gee whiz, we really should get around to changing things some day" sort of enterprise. It needs to be a fundamental priority for every individual, group, business, and institution in our society. To do this—to really change how students are educated—we need a new and very different mind-set that will allow us to discard many of the long-standing aspects of our cultural and institutional paradigms. We need to create new schools that will teach the new skills that will be necessary to function in this strange, new world. We must do what is necessary to prepare students for their tomorrows rather than our yesterdays. We can no longer feel content with serving what exists and, in fact, what has existed for decades. Rather, we must shape what can, what might, and what absolutely must be.

We must also face the fact that the world outside of education has embraced the changes much more quickly than our educational institutions have. As a consequence, there is a growing gap between the skills, knowledge, attitudes, attributes, and behaviors that most students leave our schools with now and what they need if they are going to survive, let alone thrive, in the culture of the 21st century.

What do we do about this gap? We must first recognize that just throwing more technology at the problem will not really solve things. The real issue is the paradigm paralysis of teachers, administrators, parents, and politicians, who have a rearview-mirror mentality when it comes to what schools should be. In the end, the issue is not just a hardware issue. More and more, it is a headware issue. It is about paradigm and the way we view the world. Those in education must learn to get comfortable with the inevitable and constantly coming change and use it to shape our vision of tomorrow and the tomorrows beyond tomorrow.

Windows on the Future is a challenge to all of us, especially those in education, to become actively involved in this process of change. Business management guru James Crupi's observation, in a speech to technology educators at the University of Victoria, summarizes it beautifully. He says that in times of radical change, there are three kinds of people in the world: those who make change happen, those who watch change happen, and those who do not know what hit them. Much of the education system is in this third category. Many people within the system still believe that education can and will continue on its present path and that change is something that happens to someone else. This sort of thinking leaves us with a system ripe for the picking.

As David Thornburg said at the Computer Using Educators of California Conference in May 1999, to become people who make change happen, those in the school system need to get beyond the yabbuts ("Yeah but we do not have the staff development time to help teachers learn new curriculum or to change long-standing pedagogical practices"; "Yeah but we do not have the financial resources to wire every classroom"; "Yeah but we do not yet have the resources to put all of the tools in the hands of every child"; "Yeah but we have no control over the curriculum because it is dictated by the state, by college entrance requirements, or the school board"; "Yeah but I am only a few years from retirement"). Do your colleagues get this? Does your community understand? Do your school boards, administrators, and parents have a sense of urgency about making changes to the way we prepare kids for the world after graduation?

We understand that change is hard, messy, and uncomfortable. Given this, it is easy to throw up our hands and walk away with a complete sense of hopelessness. How can we overcome this feeling? Let's digress for a moment and consider the blue whale, the largest

There is more than one way to look at the school system. Many feel that it is like a blue whale: It will take a long time for it to change direction. Maybe if we changed our point of view and saw the system like a school of herring, we would have much more hope!

mammal on earth. It is the length of three Greyhound buses placed end to end, weighs more than a fully loaded 747 jet, and has a heart almost the size of a Volkswagon Beetle. A blue whale is so big that when it decides to turn around, it can take up to 5 to 7 minutes to turn 180 degrees. Now there are a lot of people who draw a strong parallel between blue whales and schools. Both of them seem to take forever to turn around. From this perspective it seems hopeless, doesn't it?

Now it is time to shift our mind-set. Let's compare a blue whale to a school of sardines that has the same mass as the whale. Unlike the whale, a school of sardines can turn almost instantly. How do they do it? Is it ESP or a CB radio? It is neither. If you take a closer look at this phenomena, what you notice is that although all of the fish appear to be swimming together, in reality a small number of fish are beginning to swim in a different direction. As they head off on this new course, they cause conflict, friction, and collisions with the other fish, but when a critical mass of herring is reached (not a huge number such as 50% or 80% of the school but 15% to 20% who are truly committed to the new direction), the rest of the school changes direction and goes with them—almost instantaneously!

If you stop for a moment and consider some of the major recent changes in the world, you will see that huge swings in direction can happen very quickly. Isn't that exactly what happened in North America with respect to our attitudes toward smoking and toward drinking and driving? Isn't that exactly what happened in East Germany and the Soviet Union when the Communist governments lost their grip? Each of these changes were overnight successes that were years in the making and took only a small group of truly committed individuals to make happen. It is no different when we consider the necessary changes to our schools.

It is a complete myth that change takes time. It is making the decision to change that really takes the time. So where and how do we begin? By understanding that the longest journey starts with a single step—that the greatest movement starts with a single individual. This means more than using rhetoric because rhetoric alone cannot reform schools. We need action behind our words if we want real change in our schools, and this means we have to stop doing what we are doing now and start doing new things. It is up to us to take the challenge and look through the windows on the future to see our part in this great opportunity to create new schools for the new millennium.

"Change is the law of life. Those who look only to the past or the present are certain to miss the future."
                    —John Fitzgerald Kennedy

Recommended Readings⌐

The Death of Distance: How the Communications Revolution Will Change Our Lives by Frances Cairncross, Harvard Business School, 1997, ISBN: 0875848060.

Since the advent of electronic communications, there has been talk about how the world has been shrinking. Frances Cairncross, senior editor for the *Economist*, makes her case from an economical standpoint: The growing ease and speed of communication is creating a world where the miles have little to do with our ability to work or interact together. Cairncross predicts that it will not be long before people organize globally on the basis of language and three basic time shifts: one for the Americas, one for Europe, and one for East Asia and Australia. Much work that can be done on a computer can be done from anywhere. Workers can code software in one part of the world and pass it to a company hundreds of miles away that will assemble the code for marketing, and because workers can earn a living from anywhere, countries may find themselves competing for citizens as people relocate for reasons ranging from lower taxes to nicer weather. Cairncross discusses about 30 major changes likely to result from these trends, including greater self-policing of businesses, an unavoidable loss of personal privacy, and a diminishing need for countries to want emigration.

What Will Be: How the New World of Information Will Change Our Lives by Michael L. Dertouzos, Harper San Francisco, 1997, ISBN: 0062514792.

Many people have predicted what emerging technology will mean for society. Michael Dertouzos, an Internet pioneer and head of the Massachusetts Institute of Techology's Laboratory for Computer Science, has been among the few who have been pretty much right so far. Now he reaches into the coming century to paint a compelling, rationally developed picture of what is ahead. Dertouzos' fluid freedom from the Pollyanna-ism or paranoia that afflicts so many of his contemporaries brings to his visions the ring of both conviction and plausibility—and excitement as well. His clear explanations and fascinating examples are irresistible. The result is a book as enjoyable as it is important.

New Rules for the New Economy by Kevin Kelly, Penguin Group, 1998, ISBN: 0670881112.

Forget supply and demand. Forget computers. Today, communication, not computation, drives change. We are rushing into a world where connectivity is everything and where old business know-how means nothing. In this new order, success flows primarily from understanding networks, and networks have their own rules. In *New Rules for the New Economy*, Kelly presents 10 fundamental principles that invert the traditional wisdom of the industrial world. If you want to understand where the Web is heading, this book is a must.

High Tech, High Teach: Technology and Our Search for Meaning by John Naisbitt with Nana Naisbitt and Douglas Philips, Broadway Books, New York, 1999, ISBN: 0767903838.

With American culture now increasingly broadcast through technology—from television and movies to music to the Internet and electronic games—we are living in what Naisbitt calls the "Technologically Intoxicated Zone." This zone is a confusing and distracted state where we both fear and worship technology, where we see technologies as toys and quickfixes, and where we become obsessed with what is "real" and what is "fake"—from the violent games children play to genetically engineered animals to whether one can claim to have scaled Everest if supplemental oxygen was used.

Technology's saturation of American society, with its fabulous innovations and its devastating consequences, is explored by Naisbitt and his coauthors in this timely book. By consciously examining our relationship with technology as consumers of products, media, and emerging genetic technologies, we can learn to become aware of the impact technology will have on our daily lives and our children, religiosity, arts, and humanness. *High Tech,*

High Teach is a cautionary tale that shows us how to make the most of technology's benefits while minimizing its detrimental effects on our culture.

In a compelling tour of our technological immersion as we work and play and search for a spiritual path, Naisbitt tackles complex questions: Does technology free us from constraints of the physical world, or does it tie us down to our machines? Does it save time in our day-to-day lives, or does it merely create a void we feel compelled to fill with even more tasks and responsibilities? And what about advances in biotechnology? Recent developments in genetic engineering now raise the possibility of a future that will some day be free of the birth defects, disabilities, and diseases that mark our lives today. But in an age where such things are possible, what is natural and what is artificial? And when people can be created in the laboratory as easily as in the womb, what then does it truly mean to be human?

Moving from the information and machine technologies of computers, the Internet, and telecommunications to the genetic technologies that are transforming biological science and art, this book reveals the emerging power we have over our destinies and the need for a moral compass to guide us. Whether you work inside or outside of education and whether your focus is on schools or business, this is an ideal book to usher in a century in which these issues will become even more timely.

Taming the Beast: Choice & Control in the Electronic Jungle by Jason Ohler, TECHNOS Press of the Agency for Instructional Tech, 2000, ISBN: 0784208735.

Jason Ohler gets it. Twenty years and 100 billion dollars into the computer and information revolution, most people are still consumed with cards and cables, hardware and software, input and output, and RAM and ROM. In *Taming the Beast*, Ohler moves well beyond technolust and technodrool to take a hard look at the critical issues that confront us. He shows us that only by getting beyond the tool to the context of the tool and its application to the task can we ever hope to understand and control the Beast.

Taming the Beast is a rare blend of philosophical reflection, earnest wit, and hard-nosed guide. It casts a cold eye on our love-hate affair with technology; reveals 27 ways to see, evaluate, and gain control over the electronic and mechanical extensions that have become such vital parts of our lives; and shows how we can choose new machines wisely for educational, business, and community use. This book is essential reading and understanding for educators at all levels, administrators, parents, policy- and decision-makers, the media, and all citizens who recognize the extraordinary potential—and impact—of technology on education and society.

Growing Up Digital: The Rise of the Net Generation by Don Tapscott, McGraw-
Hill, 1997, ISBN: 0070633614.

This eye-opening, fact-filled book profiles the rise of the Net Generation,
which is using digital technology to change the way individuals and society
interact. Essential reading for parents, teachers, policymakers, marketers,
business leaders, social activists, and others, *Growing Up Digital* makes a
compelling distinction between the passive medium of television and the
explosion of interactive digital media, sparked by the computer and the
Internet. Tapscott shows how children, empowered by new technology, are
taking the reins from their boomer parents and making inroads into all areas
of society, including our education system, the government, and the economy. The result is a timely, revealing look at our digital future that kids and
adults will find both fascinating and instructive. Exhaustively researched
and documented, this book provides excellent insights in current trends and
future thinking from the Nintendo Generation that is poised to conquer our
world.

*If It Ain't Broke. . . Break It: And Other Unconventional Wisdom for a Changing
Business World* by Robert J. Kriegel, Louis Patler, Warner Books, 1992,
ISBN: 0446393592.

"Break-it thinkers" have proven that challenging conventional thinking
is the only way to stay ahead of the competition in the corporate environment of constant change. Kriegel shows readers how to turn the way we look
at the world upside down. This book is a guide to unlocking creative
thought in order to work smarter. It employs hundreds of real-life examples
to teach readers how to break away from the pack and apply innovative
principles to their careers.

The Infomedia Revolution: How It Is Changing Our World and Your Life by Frank
Koelsch, McGraw-Hill Ryerson, Toronto, 1995, ISBN: 007551847.

Even though this book is 5 years old, a single tiny pocket calculator is
more powerful than all the computers that existed in the world prior to 1950.
Our children's video games are more potent than the multimillion-dollar
business computers of only a few years ago. The computer's massive progress to date is just a small step in a revolution that will carry us into a star-
tlingly different future. Where the TV has failed to bring about McLuhan's
vision of a global village, millions of business and home computers connected to the World Wide Web will. The world's most power technologies—
computing, communications and media—are converging. These industries

form the largest, most dynamic and fastest growing industrial block in the world. Their collision will create Infomedia. No company or individual will escape the fallout. Infomedia will be the primary competitive weapon of the 21st century. A new generation of technology-astute companies and individuals will leverage Infomedia to achieve stellar success. The Infomedia Revolution will challenge us on a very personal level. It will raise new issues of morality, privacy, and ethics. It will change the way we work, play, entertain ourselves, and conduct our everyday lives. It will change the way our children interact with others and how they are educated. Their new world will be very different from ours.

Future Edge: Discovering the New Paradigms of Success by Joel Arthur Barker, William Morrow & Co, 1992, ISBN: 0688109365.

If you have never heard of a paradigm, this book is a good introduction to the subject. A paradigm is a thought process that simplifies our thinking incorrectly. After we become familiar with the paradigm, we have to develop a new and better paradigm to deal with the issues that the paradigm does not sufficiently address. The book focuses on how to anticipate changes in paradigms, who to look to for new paradigms, and how to take advantage of this anticipation. Of particular value is the section where Barker shares many examples of paradigm paralysis. These are brilliantly conceived, and make it easier for you to appreciate what a paradigm is. If you are committed to overcoming stalled thinking to achieve exponential success, this book is a prerequisite.

The Tipping Point: How Little Things Can Make a Big Difference by Malcolm Gladwell, Little Brown Books, 2000, ISBN: 0316316962.

Why did crime in New York drop so suddenly in the mid 90s? How does an unknown novelist end up a best-selling author? Why is teenage smoking out of control when everyone knows smoking kills? What makes TV shows like *Seame Street* so good at teaching kids how to read? Why did Paul Revere succeed in his famous warning? Equating the potential spread of mass behavior with the efficient, if deadly, spread of viruses and epidemics, Malcolm Gladwell shares his take on the ripple effect in this highly readable pop-sociology book, culled mainly from his series of articles published in *The New Yorker.* Just as a single sick person can start an epidemic of the flu, so too can a few fare-beaters and graffiti artists fuel a subway crime wave, or a satisfied customer fill the empty tables of a new restaurant. These are social epidemics, and the moment when they take off, when they reach their critical mass, is the "tipping point." Gladwell introduces us to the particular personality types that are natural pollinators of new ideas and trends—the people who create the phenomenon of word of mouth. He analyzes fashion trends, direct mail, the Internet, and the early days of the American Revolution for clues about making ideas infectious, and visits a religious commune, a successful high-tech company, and one of the world's greatest salesmen to show how to start and sustain social epidemics. Observing the behavior of these types, it's possible to trace the formation of mass social patterns, such as teenage suicide rates, the efficiency of small work units, and even the resurgence of an outdated brand-name garment. Full of challenging snippets, like his take on drug experimentation and prisons, the author's argument underscores the value of the information highway and the increased dominance and efficacy of the communication age.

The Soft Edge: A Natural History and Future of the Information Revolution by Paul Levinson, Routledge Books, 1997, ISBN: 0415157854.

According to Paul Levinson, it would be improper to portray information technology as the cause of change in our world. However, he clarifies that its role in enabling change can hardly be overestimated. He also points out, through riveting examples, that inventions have unintended consequences and uses. Why is it, for example, that the move from polytheism to monotheism failed when attempted by the pharaoh Ikhnaton, yet took solid root among the Hebrews who were taken out of Egypt by Moses only 150 years later? Levinson argues that communication technology played a key role: The awkward Egyptian hieroglyphics failed to carry the ideology as well as the Hebrew alphabetic system. From there, Levinson examines the early social changes that became possible because of what the author calls "the first digital medium": the alphabet. He considers how the Reformation, economic and political movements, and the scientific revolution were largely enabled by the printing press. He then discusses the influence of photographic communications and electronic technology such as the telegraph, the telephone, and broadcasting. He devotes the second half of the book to our present digital revolution, from word processing to the Internet and beyond. One of his key points is that new technology doesn't necessarily displace the old so much as it expands it. Therefore he doesn't see any end to using paper anytime soon. However, he sees great need for changes in the way we view creative rights. He proposes what he calls an "electronic watermark" for intellectual property—a universal patent number that will be embedded in intellectual property and will notify users in any medium of the property's creators. He puts forth his ideas in a manner that is both formal and engaging. He has a knack for making his reader feel intelligent and respected, particularly when he looks at issues of ethics and a speculative future.

What Will Be: How the New World of Information Will Change Our Lives by
Michael L. Dertouzos, Harper San Francisco, 1997, ISBN: 0062514792.

Many have predicted what emerging technology will mean for society. Michael Dertouzos, an Internet pioneer and Head of MIT's Laboratory
for Computer Science, has been among the few whose predictions have
been accurate thus far. Now he reaches into the coming century to paint a
compelling, rationally developed picture of what's ahead. Dertouzos' fluid
freedom from the Pollyanna-ism or paranoia that afflict so many of his
contemporaries brings to his visions the ring of both conviction and plausibility—and excitement as well. His crystal explanations and fascinating
examples are irresistible. The result is a book as enjoyable as it is important.

*Who Moved My Cheese? An Amazing Way to Deal With Change in Your Work and
in Your Life* by Spencer Johnson & Kenneth Blanchard, Penguin USA,
1999, ISBN: 0399144463.

With *Who Moved My Cheese?* Dr. Spencer Johnson realizes the need for
finding the language and tools to deal with change—an issue that makes all
of us nervous and uncomfortable. Most people are fearful of change because
they don't believe they have any control over how or when it happens to
them. Since change happens either *to* the individual or *by* the individual,
Spencer Johnson shows us that what matters most is the attitude we have
about change. With the start of a new millennium, most work environments
are finally recognizing the urgent need to get their computers and other
business systems up to speed and able to deal with unprecedented change.
What businesses are only just beginning to realize is that this is not enough:
There is a need to help people get ready, too. Spencer Johnson has created his
new book to do just that. The coauthor of the multimillion best-seller *The
One-Minute Manager* has written a deceptively simple story with a dramatically important message that can radically alter the way we cope with
change. *Who Moved My Cheese?* allows for common themes to become topics
for discussion and individual interpretation, takes the fear and anxiety out
of managing the future, and shows people a simple way to successfully deal
with the changing times, providing them with a method for moving ahead
with their work and lives safely and effectively.

Net.Savvy, Second Edition: Building Information Literacy in the Classroom by Ian
Jukes, Anita Dosaj, and Bruce Macdonald, Corwin Press, 2000, ISBN:
0761975659.

Realize the potential of the Internet in your classroom. This easy-to-
follow guide demonstrates a better way for students to use the Internet, and

provides teachers with the skills framework and sample lesson planners needed for teaching, learning, practicing, and mastering information in the digital era. *NetSavvy* shows you how to deal with information technology overload, solve any information challenge with six critical steps, help students harness the Web with simple techniques, create your own lesson plans using sample lesson planners, and apply frameworks for grade-level objectives and skills. Through a five-step process, the "5As of Information Literacy," both students and the most technology-resistant teachers learn to solve problems by asking, accessing, analyzing, applying, and assessing information from sources such as Internet sites, newsgroups, chat rooms, e-mail, and other electronic and non-electronic resources. From K-12 to university classrooms, *NetSavvy* is a must-have resource to build and improve information literacy skills.

References⌋

Barker, J. (1993). *Paradigms: The business of discovering the future.* New York: Harper.

Koelsch, F. (1995). *Infomedia revolution.* New York: McGraw-Hill Ryerson.

Kriegel, R. (1992). *If it ain't broke, break it.* New York: Warner Books.

Moore, G. (1965). *Electronics,* p. 43.

Moore, G. (2000, June 19). Gordon Moore q & a. *Time,* p. 99.

Senge, P. (1990). *The fifth discipline: The art and practice of the learning organization. New York: Doubleday.*

USA Today. (1999, January 19). *Tech trends.* p. B6.

USA Today. (1999, August 12). *Tech trends.* p. B7.

Wildstom, S. (1998, March 9). The search for the young and gifted. *Business Week,* p. 27.

Wildstom, S. (1998, September 14). Web phones: Now you're talking. *Business Week,* p. 83.

Wired. (1998, February). Intel advertisement. Vol. 6.02, p. 19.

Wired. (1999, February). Qwest advertisement. Vol. 7.02, p. 9.

Wired. (1999, September). Qwest advertisement. Vol. 7.09, p. 13.

Wurman, R. (1990). *Information anxiety.* Garden City, NY: Doubleday.

Index

Adaptability:
  business, 21
  educational institutions, 21
  viability and, 21
Agricultural Age, 118
Aiken, Howard, 36
Andreessen, 54
AOL, 62
ARPANET, 53
Assembly line, 29, 30
AT&T, 54, 62, 63, 78
Automated interpreted telephony,
  62
Automobile, impact on society, 15

Barker, J., 16
Bezuska, S., 18-19
Bloom's Taxonomy of Higher
  Order Thinking Skills, 98
Business Week, 77, 99

Calculators, debate over
  educational use of, 19

Career changes, 80
"Celleputer," 64, 65
Cellular phones, miniaturization
  of, 78-79
Central planning, 30
Change:
  acceleration of technological,
    43-44, 127
  as constant, 2
  as uncomfortable, 5
  key to successful, 77
  making decision to, 127
  resisting, 5
  speed of, 22-23
  subtlety of, 1
  See also Technology-driven
    change
Common school model, ix
Communication Age, 71, 87, 92
Communication skills, 96-97
  listening, 96, 97
  reading, 96
  speaking, 96, 97
  21st century, 106
  writing, 96

Compartmentalization, 29
Computational power, 43
    graph of increase in, 42, 75
    time graph of, 38-39, 40
    See also Technology
        development
Computational technology,
    history of, 33, 75
    abacus, 34
    automatic calculation devices,
        36
    counting stones, 34, 124
    electromechanical
        computational device, 35, 39
    electronic numerical integrator
        and calculator (ENIAC), 36,
        39, 41, 43, 44
    mechanical gear-based
        calculator, 34-35
    microprocessors, 37-38, 41, 43,
        53, 70
    silicon-chip computers, 37
    supercomputers, 38, 39, 124
    transistor-based computers, 36-
        37, 41
    See also Technology
        development
Computer Age, beginning of, 36
Computers:
    changing view of, 5-6
    debate over educational use of,
        19
    evolution of, 6-7
    evolution versus revolution, 10
    miniaturization of, 78
    portable, 53
    See also Computational
        technology, history of;
        Microcomputers
Contractors, using outside, 106
Control, top-down, 30
"Cookie cutter" mentality, 28, 29
Coping strategies, change and, 2
Crupi, J., 126
Curriculum:
    explicit, 120

    implicit, 120
    interrelated, 109-110
    null, 120-121
    separate-subject, 109-110
Cyberspace, 55

Daggett, W., 61
Data services, demand for, 56
Decisionmakers:
    resisting change, 24
Digital cameras, miniaturization
    of, 79
Digital watch:
    as business switch, 16
    Japanese and, 16
    Swatch, 18
    Swiss and, 16-18, 19, 21
    See also Paradigm paralysis
Digitized communication, 78
Digitized information, 78
Disability, new definition of, 89
Disney, 62
Division of labor concept, 28
DSL, 57

Eckert, Presper, 36
Edison, Thomas, 108-109
Education:
    adaptability, 21
    as key to future, 67
    as *the* major issue, 125
    catching up to technology,
        67-76
    for all ability levels, 88-89
    in Industrial Age, 29-30
    irrelevant, 73, 74, 75
    national security and, 125
    real-world relevance, 82, 107
    society and, 67
    technology revolution and,
        68-69
    train metaphor, 69-70, 72, 73,
        74

See also Educational system;
    Learning; Schools; Teachers
Educational system:
    as learning organization, 121
    educentric worldview, 72
    Industrial Age thinking in, 73
    need for new, 76
    paradigm paralysis in, 72
    place and, 78-79
    response to technology, 72-74
    stability of, 70-72
    time and, 79-81
    See also Education; Learning
Educators, 82
    as firefighters, 90
    as social workers, 69
    challenging traditional role of,
        84
    everyone as, 81-82
    fearing replacement by
        technology, 104-105
    learning new skills, 110
    shift in instructional roles, 85
    student dependency on, 93-94,
        95
    See also Educators, new roles
        for; Teaching assistants,
        nonhuman
Educators, new roles for, 85, 94,
        113, 114
    "arsonists," 90, 117
    crafters of problems, 94
    futurists, 114-115
    guides, 94, 116-117
    knowledge experts, 118-119
    learners, 121-122
    models, 119-121
    new millennium leaders, 121
    peer facilitators, 117
    process instructors, 115-116
    team learning facilitators, 117
    See also Teacher retraining
Einstein, Albert, 108
Electronic Age, beginning of, 36
Electronics magazine, 45
E-mail, 19, 54

Emerging technologies, 52
Entrepreneurs, digital, 105
Entrepreneurship skills, 106
Evaluation of students, 119, 120
    process over product, 120
    product over process, 120
Expert systems, 83

Failure:
    as teaching tool, 108-109
Familiar, lure of the, 3-5
    ideas, 5
    things, 4
    ways of doing things, 5
    worldviews, 5
Feedback, providing to students,
    94-95
Financial management, 106
Ford, Henry, 28, 29, 109
France Telecom, 62
Futurism, viii
Futurists:
    educators as, 114-115
    quarterback as, 51

Gates, Bill, 88
Gilder, G., 57
Global digital networks, 53-58,
    62, 64, 68, 73, 78, 79, 84, 124
Global village, 10
Goal setting, 106
Hawking, Stephen, 108
Hierarchical management
    structure, 30
Higher-level thinking skills, 85
    analysis, 115
    application as, 98
    evaluation, 115
    synthesis, 115
    teaching, 115-116
Hitachi PC Wallet personal
    intelligent communicator, 64
Hoff, Ted, 37
Hollerith, Herman, 35, 39

Hypermation, 61, 83, 85

Ideas, nonlinear/wild:
   generating, 108
Independent thinking, fostering,
   94
Industrial Age, 70, 71, 118
   academic success in, 86
   business, 30
   departmentalization, 110
   educational mindset, 90
   job satisfaction, 30
   large corporations, 30
   predictability, 30
   schools, 29-30
   shift to Information Age, 73
   See also Education
Industrial paradigm, 24, 28-31
   in Information Age, 31
Information Age, 71, 87, 92, 100,
   102, 118, 125
   industrial paradigm in, 31
   new paradigm for, 31
   shift from Industrial Age, 73
Information literacy, 99-102
   as survival skill, 100
   graphic design principles, 102
   new cognitive skills, 102
Integrated circuitry, 37, 45
Intel Corporation, 37, 45
   advertisement, 64
Interactive services, 63-64
International Business Machines
   (IBM), 35, 38
Internet, 53-54, 55, 56, 57, 64, 88
   debate over educational use of,
   19
   See also E-mail; World Wide Web

Japanese:
   automobile industry, 10-11
   electronic products, 77
Japan NTT, 62

Keller, Helen, 123-124
Kennedy, John Fitzgerald, 128
Knowledge-based products:
   applying, 118
   producing, 118, 119
Koelsch, F., 106
Kreigel, R., 107
Kunin, R., 80

Labor market needs,
   understanding, 92
"Ladder to success," 30
Language translation software,
   82
Law of the Photon, 57-58
Learning:
   applied, 87
   as lifelong process, 89-90, 111
   compartmentalized, 109
   content generalization versus
      content specialization, 87
   digital-based versus paper-
      based, 86
   empowerment versus
      controlling, 90, 117
   information processing versus
      memorization, 86-87
   interest-driven, 80
   just-in-case, 80
   just-in-time, 80, 81
   need-driven, 80, 81
   nonlinear versus linear, 87-88
   places, 79, 82
   process-oriented versus
      content-driven, 91-92, 116
   real-world relevance, 82, 116,
      117
   time and, 79-81, 82
   to learn, 111
   transfer, 87
   See also Education; Personal
      learning system; Process
      skills
Learning organization:
   definition, 121
   educational system as, 121

Learning webs, 88
Lucent Bell Labs, 57

Mann, Horace, ix
Mark I, 36, 41
Mass production, principles of, 28,
    29, 30, 109, 110
Mathematical literacy, 98
Mauchly, John, 36
MCI, 62
Microcomputers, 6-7, 37-38, 39, 75
Microelectronics technology, 24,
    73
Microprocessors, 37-38, 41, 43, 53,
    70
Microsoft, 62
Mindset, 2, 11, 14, 15, 31, 55, 62, 63
    challenges to, 21
    in education, 72, 76
    letting go of, 22, 76
    making radical shift in, 12, 106
    See also Mindset skills
Mindset skills, new, 107-108
Modems, 53, 64
Monomedia, 59
Moore, Gordon, 45
Moore's Law, viii, 45-49, 53, 57, 62,
    82, 83, 84, 124
Mosaic (GUI), 54
Motorola Corporation, 56
Multimedia, 59
    information literacy and, 101-
        102

National Association of Teachers,
    19
Negotiation skills, 106
NetHopper, 64
Nintendo, 62

Open classroom, 73
Organizational hierarchies,
    flattening, 9
Organized abandonment, 107

Outcome-based education, 73

Paradigm, 2, 11, 13, 15, 27, 62, 68
    children/teens' altering, 23
    children/teens' embracing, 23
    of constant/accelerating
        change, 74, 76
    power of, 13-14
    radical shift in, 12, 23-24
    real life and, 14-15
    replacing, 21
    understanding origin of
        current, 123
    unlearning, 28
    upgrading, 21, 28
    See also Mindset; Paradigm
        paralysis
Paradigm paralysis, 16-18, 24, 78,
    110, 123
    in classroom, 18-20, 72
    parents', 126
    politicians', 126
    recovering from, 18
    results of, 17
    teachers', 126
    threat of, 24
Paradigm pressure, growing,
    21-24
Paradigm self-assessment, 25-31
    "Great North American
        Paradigm Quiz," 26-27
Paramount Pictures, 62
Pascal, Blaise, 34-35
Personal computers for all, 53,
    64-65, 68, 73, 124
Personal digital assistants
    (PDAs), 65
Personal learning pathways, 88
Personal learning system, 85
Peters, T., 108
Photonics, 46
Presentation making, 106
Problem solving, 87
    effective, 115
    See also Problem solving/
        critical thinking skills

Problem solving/critical thinking
   skills, 92-96
   debriefing students, 94-95
   define task, 93-94
   design solution, 94
   do real work, 94
   empowering students, 95
   4D approach, 93-95
   real-world relevance, 95
Process skills, 91-92
   applied technical reasoning
      skills, 98-99
   communication skills, 96-97
   empowerment from, 92
   information literacy, 99-102
   mathematics, 91, 92
   new mindset skills, 107-108
   new personal skills, 105-107
   problem solving/critical
      thinking, 92-96
   reading, 91, 92
   technical reading, 97
   technical writing, 97
   using technology as tool, 102-
      105
   versus content knowledge, 91
   writing, 91, 92

Quarterback:
   educators as, 78, 114-115
   living life as, 51-52, 107, 108

Reinventing businesses, 107
Rumsberger, R., 80
Rural American Teacher, 19

Satellite systems, worldwide, 78
Satellite technologies, 57
Schools:
   concept of time in, 68
   creating new, 68, 125
   digital information in, 86
   learning technologies in, 86

teacher retraining centers in,
   114
See also Education; Educational
   system; Learning
Scientific management, 28
SEGA, 62, 63
Self-assessment skills, 106
Self-assessors, 106
Self-learners, 106
Self-marketing, 106
Self-motivators, 106
Senge, P., 121
Smart agents, 83, 84-85
"Smart functions," 70
Smith, Adam, 28
Sony, 62
Specialists, 29
Specialization, 29
Sprint, 62
Standardization of society, 28, 30
Strategic alliances, emerging, 53,
   62-64, 68, 73, 124. *See also*
   specific companies
Stress management, 106
STRETCH computer, 37, 39, 41
Student dependency, fostering
   culture of, 93-94, 95

Tabulating Machine Company, 35
Taylor, Frederick Winslow, 28
TCI, 63
Teacher retraining, 113
   impediments to, 113-114
Teachers. *See* Educators
Teaching assistants, nonhuman,
   82-85. *See also* Expert systems;
   Hypermation; Smart agents
Teamwork, 106
Technical reading skills, 97
Technical reasoning skills,
   applied, 98-99
   hands-on experiences and, 98-
      99
Technical writing skills, 97

Technological development trends:
  emerging strategic alliances (trend 3), 53, 62-64, 68, 73, 124
  global digital networks (trend 1), 53-58, 62, 64, 68, 73, 78, 79, 84, 124
  personal computers for all (trend 4), 53, 64-65, 68, 73, 124
  technological fusion (trend 2), 53, 58-62, 64, 68, 73, 124
Technological fusion, 53, 58-62, 64, 68, 73, 124
Technological overdrive, 61
Technology, 99, 118
  adults teaching, 23
  adults understanding, 23
  as tool, 102-105
  children/teens teaching, 23
  children/teens understanding, 23
  coming to terms with, 5-10
  embracing, 22
  growing comfort with, 10
  impact on modern life, 70
  learning to use, 22
  missing significance of, 15
  old mental patterns and, 9
  organized around student learning, 103
  perceived as threat, 5
  resisting, 5, 9
  rethinking, 8-10
  stepping back from, 7-8
  student learning organized around, 103
  time lag in accepting, 9-10
  transparent, 104
  understanding, 22
  versus ideas guiding use of, 5, 8
  See also Computers; Technology development; Technology-driven change
Technology-based solutions, 3

Technology development:
  acceleration of change, 39, 43-44, 68
  as exponential, 39, 40, 43, 44
  compression of, 39, 43
  See also Moore's Law; Technological development trends
Technology-driven change, 3, 5, 33-44
  as global, 10
  discomfort and, 11
  education and, 11
  global competitors and, 10-11
  power of, 10
  speed of, 10, 22-23
  workplace and, 11
Telecommunications, evolution of, 54
Telecommuting, 9
TelecomputerTV, 64
Thinking "outside the box," 108
Thornburg, D. D., 9, 88, 126
Time management skills, 106
Time Warner, 62
TQM, 73

U.S. Census, 35
U.S. Department of Labor:
  1998 statistics, 80
U.S. Weather Bureau, 37
USA Today, 56, 63

Video cameras, miniaturization of, 79
Virtual reality, 59-60
Vision, need for, 123-128
Voice recognition software, 82
  Naturally Speaking, 82
  Via Voice, 82
Voice recognition systems, 61-62

Walsh, J., 105
Whitney, Eli, 28, 109
Wired, 46, 54, 57, 61, 64
Wireless technologies, 55, 78
   demographics and, 56
Wisdom, 118

Work experience, 107
WorldCom, 62
World Wide Web, 19, 53, 54, 55,
   56, 86, 88, 89, 99-100, 101. *See
   also* Internet
Wurman, Richard, 100